Gourmet
SANDWICHES

Gourmet
SANDWICHES

SUZANNE BLYTHIN

NEW
HOLLAND

Acknowledgements

My love of food and cooking has been encouraged by the many friends and family members who have shared it with me over the years.

Thank you to each of you for the joy and pleasure of our times spent together over food, but in particular Dennis, my husband, our daughters, Hannah and Molly, and my Mum and Dad whose positive support and acknowledgement for whatever I have chosen has been unfailing.

I would also like to thank the following local businesses who generously provided assistance in the production of this book: Plenty Kitchen and Homewares, Victoire Bakery, Bakers Delight Rozelle and Rozelle Fruit and Vegetables.

This book is dedicated to John and Jean Pratt,
parents of the original inspirational sandwich.

Contents

Thai chicken meatballs and salad

Moroccan lamb balls

Baguettes   88

Vietnamese banh mi

French café

Hot dog

Tomato and brie

Panini   98

Frittata, rocket and anchovy mayonnaise

Bocconcini, tomato and pesto

Goat's cheese, rocket, and semi-dried tomato

Smoked ham, tomato and aioli

Proscuitto and provolone

Pecorino, pear and rocket

Bagels   112

SAVOURY BAGELS:

Spinach, cream cheese, roast beef and semi-dried tomato

Smoked salmon, cream cheese, dill and capers

Beef, horseradish and caramelised onion

SWEET BAGELS:

Cinnamon ricotta with bananas and honey

Chocolate, strawberry and hazlenuts

CONDIMENTS AND ACCOMPANIMENTS 218

Mayonnaise and aioli

Thousand Island dressing

Caramelised onion relish

Coleslaw

Raspberry jam

Tomato chutney

Pesto

Tomato sauce

Hoummous

Semi-dried tomatoes

Leaves and garnishes

Chargrilled /roasted vegetables

Potted beef

Introduction

This book brings the world of sandwiches to your fingertips, from high tea to picnics, from birthdays to dinner parties. Sandwiches have been the staple lunchtime meal for generations of school children and workers, and are now a significant part of the entertainment culture: finger sandwiches are the new cupcake!

Easier access to an international range of fresh breads, as well as vegetables, cheeses and meats, has elevated the humble sandwich from its lowly origins as a plate for more palatable food to the dining rooms of high society, restaurants and gourmet establishments.

Everyone has a favourite sandwich!

MY FIRST SIGNIFICANT SANDWICH

My first memory of a significant sandwich moment was during my fifth birthday party in Derbyshire. Even in 1968, we were a health-conscious family. I remember Dad layering six slices of forbidden white bread with a mix of fillings all on top of each other. He then stacked them all together, cut off the crusts (also unheard of in our house) and cut the remaining tower into small but beautiful fingers of multicoloured delight. They were spectacular, and became an essential element of every birthday party thereafter.

As my own interest in food and cooking developed, the combination of flavours and textures that work together has provided me with an endless source of pleasure, and earned me the reputation of being somewhat of a 'sandwich bore'. It became a standard joke for me to regale reluctant listeners (especially my brother-in-law) with a detailed list of ingredients in the latest sandwich combo I have discovered.

During my early twenties, I became the unofficial local caterer for weddings and parties among friends and family. I was always on the lookout for cost-efficient entertaining options and fresh bread was always an excellent base from which to begin. I discovered the many forms that the sandwich can take: open sandwiches, petite and palatable crostini, mini bagels and brioche with their particular flavour associations, pin wheels, wraps, rolls, baked fresh bread nests, croutons, layered loaves… the possibilities are endless. And delicious.

When I became a parent, I spent many hours in the kitchen preparing packed lunches for my school-aged daughters. Finding a balance of healthy, nutritious and varied food presents a constant challenge. The tediousness of this task was often alleviated by my new sandwich creations, based on leftovers, or newly discovered combinations of foods (such as my UK nephew Daniel's obsession with cheese, salami, tomato and hommus on white bread).

I have thankfully passed on my interest in food to one of my children, so was relieved of lunch-making responsibilities relatively early on in the piece. When I began managing childcare centres, I strengthened my commitment to good health and nutrition for children, teaching them about food and cooking through our daily activities. Sandwiches are often the perfect vehicle for this!

A QUICK HISTORY OF THE SANDWICH

The verb 'to sandwich' refers to the positioning of anything between two other things of different quality or character, or to put things in layers. Indeed, the definition of a sandwich in the twenty-first century is as diverse and broad as the ingredients that may go into it.

The original sandwich in medieval times was a Trencher, a slab of fresh bread used as a plate to absorb the juices of the edible food, which was then fed to the dogs or beggars.

Initially in Europe, sandwiches were the food of the lower classes, who ate them as a convenient snack during late-night gaming and drinking. Later, the sandwich appeared in more delicate forms as a supper among the aristocracy. During the 19th century, the rise of industry and the rapid, massive growth of a working-class population in Europe secured the sandwich's popularity as a cheap and portable lunchtime meal. As fresh bread became a staple of all Western diets, the sandwich gained popularity.

It is reported that the sandwich acquired its name from John Montague, fourth Earl of Sandwich, who ordered 'two bits of meat tucked between two pieces of fresh bread'. Rumour has it that eating in this manner allowed him to continue playing cards without the cards getting greasy from the meat. Others ordered 'the same as Sandwich', so the name was born.

Bread Essentials

Not all great sandwiches require freshly baked gourmet bread. Some are actually better suited to supermarket-style white or wholemeal loaves.

I use a variety of different breads from a variety of sources. It's great to have a selection of rolls, Turkish flat breads, pita breads and wraps and sliced loaves readily available so that you can always make what you hanker for.

All breads keep well in the freezer for several weeks provided they are properly wrapped. (If you buy unsliced loaves don't freeze them whole unless you intend to use the whole thing when you defrost it—frozen bread is impossible to slice!)

Speciality fresh breads are becoming more popular, and in some cases it is worth paying the extra for the improved texture and taste. Authentic French baguettes have a particular size, flavour and density that are perfect for the contents of the sandwich, and which are notably missing in other less traditional, larger and more airy baguettes. A real, fresh French baguette needs nothing extra to make it delicious, but for me, a wedge of oozing Camembert or simple butter and raspberry jam prompts nostalgia for the Parisian weekends of my twenties!

Turkish flat breads are readily available in most supermarkets, and while these have the basic elements of a Turkish loaf, I generally find them to be too doughy and thick compared to those bought directly from Turkish pide houses or bakeries. The light texture and delicate milkiness of real Turkish bread is easily complemented by suitable flavours.

Wraps come in packs of six or 10 from the supermarket, in various forms of pita breads and pockets, burritos, mountain bread and lavash. You can even get spinach, herb and tomato flavours which, to be honest, provide more visual interest than taste.

Italian bread is best bought from an Italian bakery; authentic methods of preparation and baking have a dramatic effect on the final product, and the ciabatta and pane di casa rolls and loaves available from the supermarket are rarely as tasty or distinctive as the real thing.

Panini is the Italian word for small fresh bread roll, typically ciabatta or rosetta. It describes a broad range of breads suitable for a sandwich; ask for a panini at any Italian bakery and they will show you three or four different bread rolls. In Italy, a single filled roll is actually a panino, but the word panini is now internationally recognised as an Italian-style sandwich.

Brioche is another bread variety most commonly found in France, but increasingly available in bakeries and even supermarkets. Brioche is almost cake-like in texture, since it is made with both eggs and butter and has a sweet flavour. It is excellent toasted, absorbs liquids (such as egg) well, but is also sufficiently light to make a delicate sandwich with a difference. I like to use mini brioche for canapés, as they are petite and not too weighty for delicate party food aesthetics.

Sourdough has become popular in recent years and is available in many types, shapes and flavours. Its dense texture makes it excellent for toast and ideally robust for sandwiches.

Bagels are commonly found in speciality bagel houses where they are worth purchasing. Bagels are traditionally boiled before being baked in the oven, which gives them their particular flavour and texture.

Sliced breads are available in several varieties in supermarkets, with different seeds and grains, spices, crusts and textures. Many of them are the perfect vehicle for a good sandwich.

Condiments are the backbone of a good sandwich. Mustards (a variety), mayonnaise, salad cream, olive oil, balsamic and other vinegars, sea salt and freshly ground pepper are essential ingredients. I also keep jars of olives, artichokes and grilled red capsicum as well as fig and quince pastes, pickles, pestos, chutneys and relishes in the pantry and fridge. It is these extra ingredients that take a sandwich from ordinary to excellent. The skill comes in the artful combining of flavours, and knowing which ingredients can be substituted and which are essential.

Butter is not essential for sandwiches. Sometimes mayonnaise or olive oil provide a better flavour complement for the sandwich filling. However, the oiliness of butter stops moisture from soaking into the fresh bread, minimising sogginess. I am specific in the following recipes about which need butter and which don't but you can, of course, make your own decision. Generally I prefer to use a European-style unsalted butter (Lurpak is my favourite), which has a subtle and delicate butter flavour that seems to complement any fresh bread!

Greens such as a selection of leaves, vegetables and herbs should be readily available as these provide substance, colour, texture and flavour, as well as nutritional value, to your sandwich.

Cheeses store well for several weeks if properly kept. Feta, haloumi, good tasty cheese and cream cheese are all fantastic sources of flavour and can either supplement or be the main event in a tasty sandwich. Hard cheese like parmesan, cheddars and pecorino often develop flavour as they mature, so it is important to learn to wrap and store them well to minimise waste and ensure that they become part of your everyday pantry items.

Cold meats and leftovers are often the inspiration for a sandwich and can be successfully incorporated into some interesting combinations once you have the basics available.

There is no shame in visiting a deli or supermarket and buying pre-made, chargrilled vegetables, sliced cheeses and meats to use in your sandwiches. If you want something quick and easy and cheap but still delicious, this is the way to go. I keep frozen grated parmesan, pecorino and mozzarella cheeses on hand at all times. Some cold meats can also be frozen, while many cured meats (chorizo, salami, pepperoni) can be bought in vacuum-sealed packaging and stored for weeks unopened.

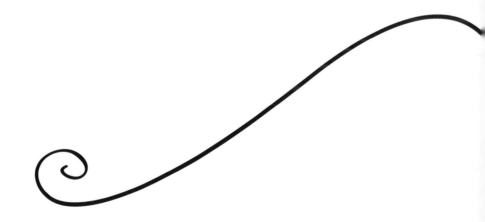

High Tea

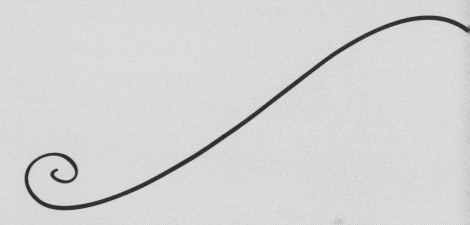

The presentation of high tea sandwiches is as important as their flavour. The arrangement, colours and delicacy of a high tea platter are integral parts of the experience.

Make sure you have china, or at least porcelain, cups and saucers in which to serve your guests tea, and offer linen napkins, crockery and side plates to enhance the elegance. Delicate cake forks and silverware are also lovely accessories.

When preparing the sandwiches, remember they are petite. Use generous amounts of fillings to ensure that the bread is not the overpowering flavour. While ensuring that each small sandwich contains plenty of filling, remember you will be trimming the crusts so don't waste ingredients by putting them right to the edges.

Finger sandwiches need to be fluffy and light, so you need an excellent bread knife to cut the sandwiches evenly and cleanly without pressing them flat. Serving a mixture of dainty triangles and elegant fingers makes an attractive platter.

Finger Sandwiches

Dainty finger sandwiches can be arranged on a tiered serving plate with others of the same type. If you want something more creative, alternate the breads according to colour or filling and create a chequerboard pattern. Large square and rectangular serving platters also look great, just check that you have the right number of sandwiches to fill the platters before you start assembling.

Egg and Cress Fingers

Everyone loves an egg sandwich. My tastiest complement to the creamy egg is mustard cress, the type that, as a child, we used to grow on wet tissues in a couple of days. Seeds can be bought from any nursery or you can buy it ready to use from a good grocer.

MAKES 6 DAINTY SANDWICHES

INGREDIENTS

2 hard-boiled eggs

1 tablespoon (20ml) mayonnaise (see Condiments)

salt and pepper

4 slices soft white fresh bread, lightly buttered

½ small punnet (approx 100g/3½oz) mustard cress

(or use finely shredded iceberg lettuce, watercress or snow pea sprouts)

METHOD

Slice and fork the eggs together with mayonnaise, salt and pepper to make a coarse mixture.

Spread evenly across two slices of fresh bread.

Top one slice with scattered mustard cress and place other slice on top.

Trim crusts off sandwich and cut into three fingers, then cut each finger in half.

Smoked Salmon, Dill and Cucumber

MAKES 6 DAINTY SANDWICHES

INGREDIENTS

1 tablespoon (20ml) whole egg mayonnaise (see Condiments)

2 teaspoons (approx 16) baby capers, chopped

1 teaspoon chopped fresh dill

4 slices soft white fresh bread, lightly buttered

50–100g (1½–3½oz) smoked salmon (or smoked trout)

¼ small or English cucumber, finely sliced

black pepper

METHOD

Combine the mayonnaise, chopped capers and dill and spread on the two slices of fresh bread.

Place the smoked salmon generously on top.

Overlap nine thin slices of cucumber until it is covering the salmon.

Season with freshly ground black pepper.

Top with second slice of fresh bread.

Trim crusts off sandwich and cut into three fingers, then cut each finger in half.

Crab, Chives and Celery

You can buy fresh crabmeat from good supermarkets and delicatessens. Frozen or tinned can also be used.

MAKES 6 DAINTY FINGERS

INGREDIENTS

¼ stick celery, very finely chopped

½ tablespoon (15g) crème fraiche

2 garlic chives (or ordinary chives), finely chopped

70g (2½oz) crabmeat

salt and black pepper

4 slices soft white bread, lightly buttered

METHOD

Mix the celery with the crème fraiche and chives.

Add the crabmeat, gently stirring to combine. Season well with salt and pepper.

Spread the mixture onto two slices of fresh bread.

Top with second slice of bread.

Trim the crusts and cut into three fingers, then cut each finger in half.

Chicken and Walnut

Chicken is such a versatile ingredient, perfect for sandwiches. The texture and flavour of shredded chicken breast is quite distinct and subtle.

MAKES 6 DAINTY FINGERS

INGREDIENTS

½ tablespoon (10g) cream cheese (softened)

½ tablespoon (10g) mayonnaise (see Condiments)

1 tablespoon (20ml) milk

a handful of walnuts, finely chopped

½ poached chicken breast (approx 100g/3½oz), shredded

1 tablespoon flat-leaf parsley, chopped

salt and black pepper

4 slices soft wholemeal fresh bread, lightly buttered

METHOD

Mix the cream cheese and mayonnaise together. If a more liquid consistency is needed to coat the chicken, add a small quantity of milk.

Stir the walnuts into the mayonnaise mixture.

Add the shredded chicken and chopped parsley, and mix to combine. Season to taste.

Divide the mixture onto two slices of fresh bread and top with the other slices.

Trim crusts off sandwich and cut into three fingers, then cut each finger in half.

Triangles & Circles

As with the fingers, the presentation of these sandwiches is all-important. A tiered plate can look beautiful when properly constructed. The neat and petite triangles and circles can also be lined up in rows of uniform fillings, or in a pattern of coloured fresh breads or fillings on a large platter.

Potted Beef Triangles

Homemade potted beef beats all the imitations. Real potted beef can be found in some butchers. It is incredibly simple to make, although it does need to cook for several hours, but it is absolutely delicious.

MAKES 8 DAINTY TRIANGLES

INGREDIENTS

2 tablespoons potted beef (see Condiments)

4 slices soft wholemeal fresh bread, not buttered

1 finely sliced cucumber

salt and black pepper

METHOD

Spread the potted beef liberally onto two slices of fresh bread.

Carefully lay thin cucumber slices on top.

Season with salt and pepper.

Top with second slice of fresh bread.

Trim the crusts and cut each into four neat triangles.

Double Brie, Quince and Rocket Triangles

You can use any soft brie or similar cheese for this sandwich. Ideally, use a fairly strongly flavoured cheese, as the quince paste and rocket are also quite strong and can overpower.

MAKES 8 DAINTY TRIANGLES

INGREDIENTS

8 slices (75g/2½oz) double brie cheese (about 5mm or ¼ thick)

4 slices soft white fresh bread, lightly buttered

a handful of baby rocket leaves

1 tablespoon quince paste (or fig, date or similar)

salt and black pepper

METHOD

Arrange the brie on two slices of fresh bread.

Add the rocket leaves sparingly.

Spread the quince paste on the second slice of fresh bread and put the two slices together.

Season with salt and pepper.

Trim the crusts and cut each into four neat triangles.

Smoked Ocean Trout with Lime Cream Cheese Triangles

MAKES 8 DAINTY TRIANGLES

INGREDIENTS

1 tablespoon softened cream cheese

2 teaspoons (10ml) whole egg mayonnaise (see Condiments)

½ lime

salt and black pepper

4 slices soft wholemeal fresh bread, lightly buttered

50–100g (1½–3½oz) smoked ocean trout

METHOD

Combine the cream cheese and mayonnaise.

Add the juice and grated peel of ½ lime. The mixture needs to be quite stiff, so do not add all the lime juice if this makes it runny.

Season with salt and pepper to taste.

Spread quite thickly onto two slices of fresh bread.

Top with slices of ocean trout and second slice of fresh bread.

Trim the crusts and cut each into four neat triangles.

Dainty Prawn Circles

These little delicacies should be served on their own circular platter——in large quantities since they will be snapped up immediately on presentation!

MAKES 15 CIRCLES

INGREDIENTS

2 tablespoons (30ml) mayonnaise (see Condiments)

2 teaspoons (10ml) tomato sauce

a dash of Worcestershire sauce

salt and black pepper

200g (6½oz) fresh peeled cooked prawns (roughly chopped, depending on the size)

10 slices of soft white sliced fresh bread, lightly buttered

½ teaspoon paprika

watercress or mustard cress, to garnish

METHOD

Combine mayonnaise, tomato sauce and Worcestershire sauce. Season with salt and pepper. This mixture must be quite stiff, otherwise it will not coat the prawns and will make a soggy sandwich.

Add prawns and stir gently to coat.

Cut three circles out of each slice of bread using a 4cm (1½in) cookie cutter (serrated is best for a pretty edge).

Spread 2 teaspoons prawn mixture onto 15 circles. Sprinkle each with paprika.

Top with remaining fresh bread circles.

Arrange on a large platter, garnished with watercress or mustard cress.

Entertaining

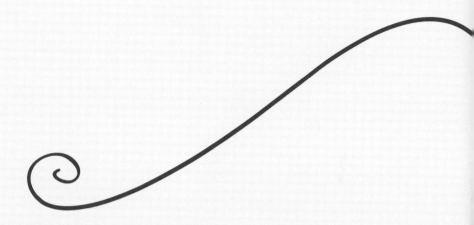

Mini brioche, bagels and crostini are perfect for your canapé menu. They are quick and easy to prepare, with much of the work done well in advance and assembled at the last minute. They are filling, easy to eat and delicious.

I prepare all the mayonnaises, dressings and spreads well in advance, and keep them in sealed containers in the fridge. Then I prepare all the ingredients stored in separate containers that have been labelled.

I make up one platter to begin with. As the evening goes on, it is usually easy to find someone who is happy to lend a hand putting the combinations together as the demand increases. This way, they are always freshly made and don't become soggy or dry around the edges.

Any unused bagels or brioche can be stored in the freezer for the next event!

Smoked Rainbow Trout with Lime Mayonnaise Open Bagel

Smoked whole rainbow trout can be bought in fishmongers and some supermarkets as well as delicatessens.

MAKES 12 HALVES

INGREDIENTS

2 tablespoons (50g) cream cheese

2 tablespoons (30ml) of lime mayonnaise (see Condiments)

6 mini bagels, halved

salt and black pepper

1 whole smoked rainbow trout, separated from bones and skin and broken into irregular chunks

finely grated zest of 1 lime

sprigs of fresh dill, to garnish

METHOD

Combine the cream cheese with the lime mayonnaise (see Condiments) and spread evenly onto the 12 bagel halves. Season with salt and pepper.

Top with chunks of rainbow trout.

Sprinkle with lime zest and a small sprig of fresh dill.

Serve on a large platter.

Smoked Turkey, Rocket and Cranberry Open Bagel

MAKES 12 HALVES

INGREDIENTS

1 tablespoon (20ml) whole egg mayonnaise (see Condiments)

12 slices (approx 200g, 6½oz) smoked turkey

6 mini bagels, halved

salt and black pepper

2 tablespoons cranberry jelly

a handful of baby rocket leaves

METHOD

Spread the mayonnaise evenly on each bagel half.

Put a slice of folded turkey on each bagel.

Season well with salt and black pepper.

Smear a teaspoon of cranberry jelly across the turkey.

Top with a few leaves of rocket (about 5 on each).

Serve on a large platter.

Blue Cheese with Caramelised Onion Open Bagel

MAKES 12 HALVES

INGREDIENTS

Caramelised onion (see Condiments)

6 mini bagels, halved

200g (6½oz) blue cheese (stilton, gorgonzola, blue brie etc.)

a few sprigs of fresh thyme

METHOD

Spread a dessertspoon of caramelised onion across each bagel half.

Slice the cheese and break it up roughly on top of the onion.

Sprinkle with thyme leaves.

Serve on a large platter.

Beef, Horseradish, Spinach and Roasted Capsicum Open Bagel

The roasted red capsicum gives a lovely sweetness to these flavoursome and substantial nibbles.

MAKES 12 HALVES

INGREDIENTS

1 red capsicum (roasted, with blackened skin peeled off)

2 teaspoons (10ml) horseradish cream (or sour cream with fresh horseradish grated into it)

2 tablespoons/50g cream cheese

6 mini bagels, halved

24–30 baby English spinach leaves

12 slices (approx 200g/6½oz) rare roast beef, finely sliced

salt and pepper

METHOD

Slice the roasted red capsicum into thin strips.

Combine cream cheese with horseradish cream.

Spread approx 1 teaspoon horseradish cream cheese on each bagel half.

Top with 2–3 baby spinach leaves.

Arrange a slice of folded beef on each and top with two or three small strips of roasted capsicum.

Season with salt and freshly ground black pepper.

Serve on a large platter.

Gruyere and Smoked Ham with Tomato Brioche

The lovely sweet nuttiness of gruyere provides a contrast to the smoked ham and sweet fresh bread and tomato. If you prefer a milder cheese, jarlsberg or edam also work well.

MAKES 16 BRIOCHE SLICES

INGREDIENTS

100g (3½oz) gruyere cheese, sliced

4 mini brioche, sliced into 4 rounds

6 shaved slices (approx 100g, 3½oz) smoked ham

2–3 vine-ripened tomatoes, thinly sliced

salt and pepper

1 tablespoon (25ml) olive oil

fresh oregano leaves (or mini basil leaves)

METHOD

Place the cheese slices onto the brioche and top with a piece of curled ham and one slice of tomato.

Season with salt and ground black pepper.

Drizzle with olive oil.

Garnish with fresh oregano leaves.

Goat's Cheese and Roasted Pumpkin Brioche

Leaving the roasted pumpkin irregularly mashed, and crumbling the cheese rather than neatly slicing, gives additional texture that is also visually interesting. Use a sweet, thick and rich vinegar to highlight the flavours of the goat's cheese and sweet pumpkin.

MAKES 12 BRIOCHE HALVES

INGREDIENTS

150g (5oz) roast butternut pumpkin

olive oil

6 mini brioche

100g (3½oz) goat's cheese, roughly cut into 12 slices

balsamic vinegar (a few drops, for drizzling)

2 bunches of fresh baby basil leaves

METHOD

Chop pumpkin into 2cm (¾in) cubes.

Par boil for 10 minutes, until beginning to soften.

Drain well.

Spray lightly with olive oil and put into a very hot oven for about 15 minutes, or until crisp and browning at the edges.

Roughly mash 3–4 pumpkin pieces onto each brioche.

Crumble goat's cheese on top.

Drizzle with balsamic vinegar and top with 2–3 baby basil leaves.

Rare Roast Beef with Semi-dried Tomato and Honey Seeded Mustard Brioche

MAKES 12 HALVES

INGREDIENTS

- 2 tablespoons (30ml) seeded mustard
- 2 teaspoons honey
- 6 mini brioche
- 12 slices (approx 200g, 6½oz) shaved rare roast beef
- 24 pieces semi-dried tomato (see Condiments)
- 2 stalks continental parsley

METHOD

Combine mustard with honey.

Spread each brioche half with mustard/honey mix.

Top with a slice of beef and 2 pieces of semi-dried tomato.

Garnish with sprigs of continental parsley.

Topped Crostini

Crostini are made with baguettes or other small bread rolls, sliced into rounds and cooked to create a small crisp base. The appearance of the crostini is enhanced by the careful use of mini ingredients like baby herbs and cherry tomatoes.

MAKES 20

INGREDIENTS

one small baguette

olive oil

METHOD

Slice a small baguette into rounds about ½cm (¼in) thick, and lightly spray each side with olive oil. Place on a baking sheet and cook in a moderate oven for about 20 minutes until golden brown.

Avocado, Pesto and Tomato Crostini

MAKES 20

INGREDIENTS

pesto (see Condiments)
1 avocado, thickly sliced and cut into large dice
10 cherry tomatoes, cut into 4 slices each
salt and black pepper
small basil leaves (pinched from the tips of the bunch)

METHOD

Roughly spread each crostini with pesto.

Arrange avocado and 2 slices of tomato on each and season well.

Garnish with a mini basil leaf.

Gorgonzola and Honey Crostini

INGREDIENTS

200g (6½oz) gorgonzola cheese, at room temperature
¼ cup (50ml) honey, to drizzle
thyme flowers and leaves

METHOD

Spread a smear of soft gorgonzola on each crostini.

Drizzle each with honey and sprinkle with thyme leaves and flowers.

Blue Cheese, Date and Walnut Crostini

INGREDIENTS

200g (6½oz) blue cheese (blue castella, blue stilton, gorgonzola, cambazola)

10 fresh dates, halved lengthways

20 walnuts, chopped roughly

METHOD

Slice the cheese and press a piece onto each crostini.

Top with half a date, flat side down, and sprinkle with chopped walnuts.

Cheddar Cheese, Caramelised Onion and Salami Crostini

MAKES 20

INGREDIENTS

20 small (or halved) slices (approx 200g, 6½oz) salami

200g (6½oz) mature cheddar cheese

6 tablespoons caramelised onion (see Condiments)

1 medium red chilli, finely sliced into rings

METHOD

Lay the salami onto the crostini.

Top with a rough slice of cheddar cheese.

Mound a teaspoon of caramelised onion on top.

Garnish with a couple of rings of red chilli.

Goat's Cheese, Roasted Pumpkin and Coriander Crostini

MAKES 20

INGREDIENTS

2 teaspoons ground cumin

2 teaspoons ground coriander

½ roast butternut pumpkin, cubed and roughly mashed (see Condiments)

salt and pepper

100g (3½oz) softened goat's cheese (or cream cheese)

a bunch of fresh coriander

METHOD

Gently toast the ground spices in a dry frying pan for about 1 minute, or until aromas intensify.

Combine pumpkin with the cooked spices and season well with salt and pepper.

Spread the goat's/cream cheese liberally onto each crostini.

Top with roughly mashed pumpkin.

Garnish with several coriander leaves.

Ricotta, Tomato and Sage Crostini

INGREDIENTS

I small bunch of fresh sage
50g (½-2oz) butter
200g (6½oz) ricotta cheese
Raspberry vinegar, or other sweet vinegar, to drizzle
5 mini Roma tomatoes
Salt and pepper

METHOD

Fry 40 individual sage leaves with melted butter in a frying pan, reserve the butter.

Spread each crostini thickly with ricotta cheese. Drizzle with sweet raspberry vinegar.

Slice the tomatoes finely and place one slice on each crostini.

Season well with salt and black pepper.

Garnish each crostini with a sage leaf and drizzle with a little of the butter.

Blue Cheese, Date and Walnut
Crostini (above), Ricotta, Tomato
And Sage Crostin (left)i

Almond and Raspberry Dessert Sandwich

These petite sweet sandwiches are lovely to serve as a dessert canapés. The raspberry tartness offsets the intense sweetness of the biscuits and the ooze and juiciness of the cream and raspberry together makes the perfect decadent finish.

MAKES 20

INGREDIENTS

1 tub (250g, 8oz) mascarpone cheese

25g (1oz) icing sugar

a few drops of vanilla extract

40 amaretti biscuits

20 raspberries (fresh will hold their shape better, but frozen can be used if handled carefully)

flaked and whole almonds, to serve

METHOD

Combine the mascarpone, icing sugar and vanilla extract (this can be substituted with amaretto liqueur if preferred).

Match the biscuits in size in twos to make even sandwiches.

Gently spread a thick layer of the mascarpone mixture onto one of the halves and top with a raspberry. Gently press the top biscuit onto the raspberry until the cream begins to ooze slightly.

Serve on a platter covered with flaked and whole almonds.

Assorted Wraps and Rolls

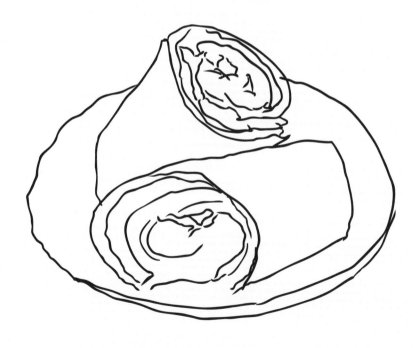

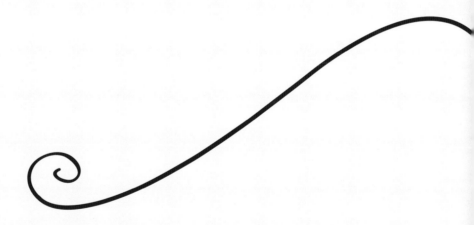

These rolls are perfect for a special occasion, or to serve a larger number of people accompanied by a salad or fries.

Combinations of the different wraps (two or three of each, cut into sections) look great on a large serving platter and easily serve 10–12 people.

Wraps and Pita

Slow Roast Lamb, Spinach, Mint, Roast Pumpkin and Feta Wrap

This is a great way to use up leftovers from a leg of lamb. If you want a delicious but quick and easy lunch for 12–15 people, a whole leg of lamb can be prepared just for this recipe. Increase the quantities of the other ingredients accordingly.

SERVES 2

INGREDIENTS

Small handful of warm slow roast lamb per person (about 50g, 1½oz)

20 baby spinach leaves, plus extra for garnish

20 mint leaves, plus extra for garnish

2 teaspoons (10ml) bottled mint jelly

1 teaspoon (5ml) olive oil

1 teaspoon (5ml) balsamic vinegar

30g (1oz) crumbled feta cheese

12 cubes of roast pumpkin (see Condiments)

2 pita pockets or Lebanese flat breads

METHOD

If using leftover lamb, warm it by sprinkling with water (this will keep it moist) wrapping it tightly in foil, and putting in a low oven (120ffC, 250ffF) for 20 minutes. Otherwise, put a whole leg in a preheated oven (140ffC, 275ffF) with 4cm (2½in) of water in a roasting tray and tightly seal with foil. Cook for at least 5 hours on a low heat (or overnight). Take out of the oven and leave to stand for at least 20 minutes.

Gently pull apart the meat while still warm and serve immediately.

Combine the salad (mint and spinach) leaves.

Combine mint jelly, oil and vinegar and pour over salad ingredients, toss gently to coat.

Crumble the feta cheese into the salad mix.

Add roasted pumpkin and the warmed lamb last. This will warm the rest of the ingredients and slightly melt the cheese.

Divide the filling into two and set out the bread or pockets. Lay the ingredients in a line down the middle third of the flat bread or put directly into the pocket.

Begin with the closest edge to the filling and wrap tightly. Cut into two across the diagonal.

Serve garnished with spinach and mint leaves.

See picture previous page

Chargrilled Vegetables with Haloumi Wrap

SERVES 2

INGREDIENTS

olive oil

90g/3oz haloumi cheese, thickly sliced

selection of chargrilled or roasted vegetables such as zucchini, eggplant, onion, fennel, carrot, pumpkin, capsicum, sliced to a thickness of ½cm (¼in) (see Condiments)

1 tablespoon natural yoghurt (Greek style)

3–4 cloves roasted garlic

2 wraps (burrito style)

20 baby English spinach leaves

salt and black pepper

mixed leaves, to serve

METHOD

Lightly spray a shallow frying pan or griddle with olive oil then heat. Grill the haloumi until lightly browned on each side. Put aside.

Prepare the vegetables (or use chargrilled vegetables purchased from a deli).

Combine squeezed roasted garlic cloves with yoghurt and season with salt and pepper.

Smear about a teaspoon of yoghurt along the bottom third of the wrap. Place a line of spinach leaves along the yoghurt. Place 3–4 slices of haloumi on top of the spinach and then arrange the roasted vegetables on top.

Season with salt and pepper and wrap tightly. Cut on the diagonal into half or thirds. Serve with mixed leaves.

Thai Beef and Salad Wrap

SERVES 2

INGREDIENTS

1 tablespoon natural yoghurt (Greek style)

½ tablespoon sweet chilli sauce

2 wraps (burrito style)

10 English spinach leaves

8 slices (approx 150g, 5oz) rare roast beef

½ long cucumber, sliced lengthways and cut into 3cm (½in) sticks

½ red capsicum, julienned

2 spring onions, finely sliced or julienned

2 stems coriander leaves, plus extra to garnish

salt and black pepper

12 mint leaves, plus extra to garnish

METHOD

Combine the yoghurt and sweet chilli sauce.

Spread each wrap generously with the yoghurt mixture.

Arrange the spinach along the bottom third of the wrap.

Top with the beef slices, cucumber, capsicum sticks, onion slices, coriander and mint leaves.

Season with salt and pepper and wrap tightly.

Cut on the diagonal into two and serve garnished with coriander and mint sprigs.

Thai Chicken Meatballs and Salad Wrap

These meatballs can be eaten as a main meal but are so quick, easy and tasty that they work really well in a wrap or sandwich.

FOR THE MEATBALLS

¼ bunch coriander leaves and stems

200g (7oz) chicken mince

1 clove of garlic, crushed

½ teaspoon each ground cumin, ginger and coriander

3 teaspoons (10ml) soy sauce

3 spring onions, finely chopped

salt and black pepper

FOR THE SALAD

½ tablespoon sweet chilli sauce

1 tablespoon (20ml) natural yoghurt (Greek style)

¼ shredded Chinese cabbage

12 mint leaves

¼ bunch fresh coriander leaves

½ Lebanese cucumber, grated and squeezed

2 spring onions, finely sliced

¼ red capsicum, finely sliced into strips

MEATBALLS

Chop a quarter of the fresh coriander leaves and stems finely.

Combine chopped coriander with the chicken mince, garlic, spices, soy sauce and spring onions. Mix thoroughly.

Season well with salt and pepper and roll into walnut sized balls. (Should make about 10 balls.)

Flatten the balls slightly and shallow fry for approximately 4 minutes on each side, until golden brown and cooked through.

Mix the sweet chilli sauce and Greek yoghurt together and spread evenly onto each wrap.

Combine the salad ingredients—cabbage, mint leaves, coriander leaves, cucumber, capsicum and shallots—and mix together well.

Lay salad onto the wrap in a line.

Top with 3–4 chicken balls. Wrap tightly and serve warm.

Moroccan Lamb Balls and Fatoush Wrap

The lamb balls can be made in much larger quantities, rolled and then frozen. If you freeze them in groups of 5, you have them easily on hand for cooking and using at any time. They can also be served on sticks as a canapÉ with a simple minted yoghurt dip.

SERVES 2

INGREDIENTS

2 pita pockets or wraps

FOR THE MEATBALLS:

2 spring onions, finely sliced

1 clove of garlic, finely chopped

200g (3½oz) lamb mince

½ teaspoon cinnamon

1 teaspoon each of ground cumin and coriander

1 tablespoon semolina

salt and pepper

olive oil

FOR THE FATOUSH:

2 tomatoes, chopped

1 long cucumber, chopped

½ red onion, finely chopped

a handful mint leaves, torn

a handful flat-leaf parsley leaves, roughly chopped

FOR THE DRESSING:

1 tablespoon olive oil

juice of ½ lemon

½ clove of garlic, finely chopped

METHOD

Combine all the meatball ingredients and mix well.

With wet hands, roll into 2½cm (1in) balls (should make around 12 balls.)

Using a small amount of olive oil, shallow fry the balls, gently browning on each side. (Takes about 5 minutes.)

If you are not in a hurry, the balls can be oven baked. Place onto a lightly greased baking sheet and cook, uncovered, in a moderate oven for 25 minutes.

Combine all the fatoush (salad) ingredients and dress with the combined oil, lemon juice and garlic, just before assembling the sandwich.

When the meatballs are cooked, allow them to cool slightly while you fill each pita pocket with fatoush.

Add the balls to the pocket, distributing evenly into the salad.

Serve warm, garnished with flat-leaf parsley and mint leaves.

Baguettes

Vietnamese Banh Mì

Banh mi is the Vietnamese version of the French salad baguette, combining ingredients introduced by the French with traditional Vietnamese ingredients like coriander, chillies, fish sauce and pickled vegetables. The pickled vegetables are available in jars from Chinese/Thai/Vietnamese specialty food shops. Some of the ingredients are not what you may typically have in your pantry, but once you have tasted these, you will make sure you do!

SERVES 2

INGREDIENTS

2 demi baguettes or ½ full-length baguette, split lengthways

2 teaspoons mayonnaise (see Condiments)

25g (2/3oz) pork liver pate

1 cucumber, peeled and sliced lengthways into 6 sheets

4 thin slices of roast pork

4 slices of pork brawn (available from delis)

sprinkling of fish sauce

4 fresh red chillies, stems removed and sliced in half

Vietnamese sweet pickled carrot and dakon or julienned sticks of carrot and spring onion drained if using bottled

6 sprigs of fresh coriander or cilantro

METHOD

Spread the top half of each baguette with a thin layer of mayonnaise (see Condiments) and the bottom half with pate.

Place 3 slices of cucumber inside each baguette.

Place 2 slices each of the pork and brawn inside each baguette and sprinkle with fish sauce.

Add finely chopped chillies.

Drain the pickled vegetables well and arrange on top of the meats.

Add generous sprigs of coriander and close (slice into 3 if using a full baguette).

See picture previous page

French Cafe Baguette

This sandwich is found in all French cafes, and is generally eaten on the run for breakfast, lunch or a quick snack. Assembling the sandwich well in advance seems to enhance the flavours. You must find a good (preferably French) baguette that is not too doughy or thick, as the success of this sandwich depends on the fillings being the main event. The simple combination of flavours—egg, tomato, ham—is mouthwateringly delicious.

SERVES 2

INGREDIENTS

2 half baguettes or 1 large baguette, cut into 15cm (6in) sections

1 tablespoon (20ml) mayonnaise (see Condiments)

1 teaspoon Dijon mustard

2 slices of leg ham off the bone (approx 30g/1oz, per slice)

1 hard boiled egg, sliced

1 tomato, sliced

salt and pepper

¼ shredded iceberg lettuce

METHOD

Halve the baguette and spread one side generously with the mayonnaise, and the other side more lightly with mustard.

Place a slice of ham on the mustard side of the baguette.

Top with slices of boiled egg (share the yolk evenly!) and tomato.

Season well with salt and pepper.

Arrange the lettuce generously on top, ensuring that the tomato slices are well covered.

Top with the other half of the baguette.

Wrap in plastic wrap or foil and refrigerate before eating—if you can wait!

Hot Dog Baguette

I first found these in the Gare de Lyon and was ridiculously impressed with the ingenious idea of creating a hole in the baguette so that the sausage stays neatly inside rather than threatening to drop out all the time! The trick is in managing to get the onions evenly inside the hole.

SERVES 2

INGREDIENTS

1 sliced onion

olive oil

2 pork sausages (choose your favourite variety, or even frankfurts will do)

1 French baguette (find a thin one as close to a real French-style baguette as possible, otherwise this becomes a very bready hot dog)

Dijon mustard

METHOD

Fry the onion gently in a teaspoon of olive oil until soft (at least 5 minutes).

Cook the sausages by barbecue, grilling or pan-frying. If using frankfurts, heat in brine or water and drain.

Cut the baguette into sausage lengths.

Create a hole down the centre of the baguette by using a metal skewer in ever increasing circles to flatten the bread towards the crusts.

Smear the sausage with Dijon mustard.

Drop some cooked onions into the hole in the fresh bread and then insert the mustard covered sausage.

Serve immediately with a serviette wrap and a French flag if you have one!

Tomato and Brie Baguette

Sometimes the simple combinations are the best. Make sure you use a good ripe brie and well flavoured tomatoes.

SERVES 2

INGREDIENTS

2 pieces of baguette

100g (3½oz) brie, at room temperature

2 tomatoes (vine-ripened or Roma), sliced thickly

salt and pepper

olive oil, to drizzle

balsamic vinegar, to drizzle

8 basil leaves

METHOD

Split the baguette horizontally on an angle.

Arrange the brie on the bottom half of the bread.

Top with the sliced tomato.

Season well with salt and pepper.

Drizzle with olive oil and balsamic vinegar.

Sprinkle with torn basil leaves.

Panini

Panini are sometimes served hot by being pressed in a grill or sandwich press. The following simple pairings of cured meats, cheeses and fresh herbs and vegies drizzled with olive oil are the essence of Italian cuisine, and make an easy but completely satisfying sandwich. Always use a fresh extra virgin olive oil.

Frittata, Rocket and Anchovy Mayonnaise Panini

Every time there are leftovers in my house, my family jokingly quips 'I'll make a frittata'. And why not? Frittatas are extremely healthy, protein-rich and versatile. They can be filled with virtually anything and served hot, warm or cold. I suggest making a large frittata for lunch and use the remainder for sandwich filings.

SERVES 2

INGREDIENTS

2 small cooked potatoes, sliced thickly

1 red onion, finely chopped or sliced

olive oil

a handful baby spinach leaves (optional)

6 eggs

salt and pepper

50ml (1¾fl oz) milk or cream

3-4 bunches flat-leaf parsley

50g (1½oz) shredded mozzarella cheese

2 panini (rosetta or ciabatta rolls)

3–6 slices of frittata

a handful of rocket leaves or arugula, plus extra for garnish

anchovy mayonnaise (see Condiments)

salt and black pepper

METHOD

Make the frittata: Slice the cooked potato and layer it into a greased oven-proof shallow dish (approximately 2 litre capacity).

Cook the onions in a small amount of olive oil until soft. Add to the potato. Sprinkle over baby spinach leaves (if using).

Whisk the eggs and season well. Add the milk or cream.

Chop and add parsley to the egg mixture.

Pour the eggs over the potatoes.

Sprinkle with shredded mozzarella cheese.

Cook in a moderate oven (200·C, 400·F, gas mark 6) for approx 20 minutes until top is golden brown and eggs firm.

Halve the rolls horizontally and butter one side lightly.

Slice the frittata into 1cm (¾in) thick pieces and arrange 2–3 slices inside each roll.

Sprinkle on the rocket leaves or arugula.

Spread the other half of the roll with 2 teaspoons of anchovy mayonnaise.

Season well with salt and black pepper.

Press the two halves well together and serve with some extra rocket leaves.

See picture on previous page.

Bocconcini, Tomato and Pesto Panini

Bocconcini are baby mozzarella cheeses. You can substitute these for mozzarella balls, which can be cut into the correct sized pieces for the bread.

SERVES 2

INGREDIENTS

2 panini (rosetta or ciabatta rolls)

1 tablespoon pesto (see Condiments)

2 Roma tomatoes, sliced

6 sliced bocconcini

olive oil, to drizzle

salt and pepper

METHOD

Halve the panini horizontally.

Spread one half of each roll with pesto.

Layer on tomato slices and then the bocconcini.

Drizzle with olive oil and season.

Goat's Cheese, Rocket, and Semi-dried Tomato Panini

Goat's cheese is readily available and there are numerous variations. The rich and distinctively creamy pre-packaged cylinders are versatile, and perfect for spreading on a sandwich.

SERVES 2

INGREDIENTS

2 panini (rosetta or ciabatta rolls)

60g (2oz) goat's cheese

6–8 semi-dried tomato wedges (see Condiments)

salt and pepper

10 rocket leaves

olive oil, to drizzle

METHOD

Halve the panini horizontally.

Spread one half of each roll with goat's cheese.

Layer on tomato wedges.

Season with salt and pepper.

Add rocket leaves.

Drizzle with olive oil.

Ham, Tomato and Aioli Panini

INGREDIENTS

- 2 panini (rosetta or ciabatta rolls)
- 1 tablespoon (20ml) aioli (see Condiments)
- 2 thick slices of leg ham (approx 40g, 1¼oz per slice)
- 2 tomatoes, sliced and drizzled with olive oil
- salt and black pepper
- olive oil
- rocket leaves, to garnish

METHOD

Halve the panini horizontally.

Spread one half of each roll generously with aioli.

Layer on ham slices and tomato.

Season with salt and pepper and drizzle with olive oil.

Top with second half of each roll.

Serve with rocket leaves.

Prosciutto and Provolone Panini

SERVES 2

INGREDIENTS

2 panini (rosetta or ciabatta rolls)

butter

4 slices provolone cheese

4 slices prosciutto

2 Roma tomatoes, sliced

salt and black pepper

olive oil, to drizzle

8–10 fresh basil leaves

METHOD

Halve the rolls horizontally and butter each side lightly.

Lay the sliced cheese and meat on one half of the roll and top with sliced tomato.

Season well with salt and black pepper and drizzle with olive oil.

Tear the basil leaves on top of the tomato and top with the second half of the roll.

Pecorino, Pear and Rocket Panini

SERVES 2

INGREDIENTS

2 panini (rosetta or ciabatta rolls)
butter
50g (1½oz) shaved pecorino
1 pear (ripe but still hard), sliced
one large handful rocket leaves
olive oil, to drizzle
balsamic vinegar, to drizzle
salt and black pepper

METHOD

Halve the rolls horizontally and butter one side lightly.

Lay the sliced cheese and pear on one half of the roll.

Top with rocket leaves.

Drizzle with olive oil and sweet balsamic vinegar.

Season well with salt and black pepper.

Top with second half of each roll.

Bagels

Bagels need plenty of strong flavours if you want to taste something other than the bread itself. As they are quite dense, they are often eaten as halves.

Spinach, Cream Cheese, Roast Beef and Semi-dried Tomato Bagel

SERVES 2

INGREDIENTS

2 bagels, sliced in half lengthways

40g (1½oz) cream cheese

6 English spinach leaves

6 slices (100g/3½oz) rare roast beef

4–6 semi-dried tomato wedges

salt and pepper

METHOD

Spread cream cheese thickly on each side of the bagels.

Layer the spinach leaves and roast beef.

Top with several tomato wedges and season well with salt and pepper.

Smoked Salmon, Cream Cheese, Dill and Capers Bagel

SERVES 2

INGREDIENTS

40g (1¼oz) cream cheese

2 bagels, sliced in half horizontally

Approximately 12 baby capers

Fresh dill

50g (1½oz) smoked salmon

¼ red onion, very finely sliced

METHOD

Spread cream cheese thickly on each side of the bagels.

Sprinkle with baby capers and fresh dill.

Divide smoked salmon between the two bagels and arrange on two halves.

Top with 3–4 slices red onion and the other half of the bagel.

Beef, Horseradish and Caramelised Onion Bagel

SERVES 2

INGREDIENTS

2 bagels, sliced in half lengthways

butter

1 teaspoon horseradish cream (or fresh horseradish finely grated with 1 tablespoon sour cream)

6 slices (approx 100g, 3½oz) rare roast beef

1 tablespoon caramelised onion (see Condiments)

a handful of rocket or arugula leaves

¼ red onion, to garnish

METHOD

Butter one half of each bagel.

Spread the horseradish cream on the other side of the bagels.

Divide the roast beef between each bagel and spread caramelised onion relish on top.

Top with rocket or arugula leaves.

Serve with slices of red onion and an extra dollop of horseradish cream.

Cinnamon Ricotta Bagel with Bananas and Honey

A delicious breakfast treat.

SERVES 2

INGREDIENTS

125g soft ricotta cheese (½ tub)

1 teaspoon ground cinnamon

1 tablespoon honey or maple syrup

1 banana, sliced on the diagonal

½ a lemon

2 bagels, sliced in half lengthways

½ tablespoon icing sugar

METHOD

Mix the ricotta with ½ teaspoon of the cinnamon and a drizzle of honey or maple syrup. Taste for sweetness.

Slice the banana and squeeze the lemon juice over it.

Toast the bagels on the open sides only.

Spread the ricotta lavishly and lumpishly on the bagel, and top with banana slices.

Drizzle remaining honey or maple syrup over the slices. Sprinkle with sifted icing sugar and remaining ground cinnamon.

Chocolate, Strawberry and Hazelnut Bagel

Who can resist the heady combination of chocolate, nuts and strawberries?

SERVES 2

INGREDIENTS

10 whole hazelnuts

2 bagels, sliced in half lengthways

1 tablespoon chocolate and hazelnut spread (for example Nutella)

3–4 strawberries, sliced thickly

mint sprigs, for garnish

icing sugar for dusting

approx 20g (4 squares) good quality dark chocolate

METHOD

Dry roast the hazelnuts in the oven (200·C, 400·F, gas mark 6) for about 10 minutes until lightly browned.

Leave to cool and then chop roughly.

Spread each half bagel smoothly with chocolate spread.

Arrange sliced strawberries and top with hazelnuts.

Garnish with a sprig of mint and dust with sifted icing sugar.

Serve with chocolate dipped strawberries for an extra special treat.

Children and Party Food

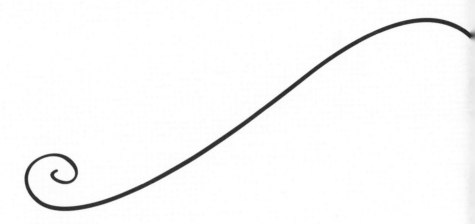

Sandwiches are ideal, nutritious daily lunchbox fillers. When deciding what to offer each day, you need to consider what your child will eat (or swap!), as well as the capacity of the sandwich to withstand temperature, being jostled inside a lunch box and ignored until it's the last resort.

If you make a delicious sandwich it will be the first thing your child reaches for, which is ideal if it contains all the nutrition your child needs for the day's activities.

Many children's tastes are becoming sophisticated as they experience food from a wide range of cultures. Any of the sandwiches in this book are suitable for children, but it is their presentation, appeal and key ingredients that guarantee they will be eaten!

Party Food

Birthday Party Fingers

These colourful multi-layered fingers are unexpectedly delicious! Don't be tempted to omit any of the layers until you have tried them in their complete form, only then are you allowed to add and subtract! Sandwich spread is an English condiment bought in jars and commonly available.

MAKES 12

INGREDIENTS

14 slices of white sliced bread

butter

1 tablespoon crunchy peanut butter

1 tablespoon cheese spread (or 1 cheese triangle)

1 tablespoon sandwich spread

Marmite (sorry, Vegemite just won't do!)

8 thin slices cucumber

4 slices beetroot, drained and halved

METHOD

Spread the fresh bread as follows: 2 with peanut butter, 2 with cheese spread, 2 with sandwich spread.

Butter the remaining slices and top 2 each with cucumber slices and beetroot slices.

Assemble the layers starting with the heavier ingredients at the bottom as follows: beetroot, cheese spread, cucumber, peanut butter, sandwich spread, Marmite.

Top with the remaining slices. Chill slightly in the fridge for about half an hour. This makes it easier to cut neatly.

Trim the crusts and cut into half and then into thirds, to make neat fingers.

Arrange on a tiered plate as for high tea at the Ritz!

Fairy Circles and Stars

These are a slightly more time consuming departure from the traditional fairy fresh bread but so much more appealing without the crusts and in delicate shapes.

MAKES 15

INGREDIENTS

Butter, softened

5 slices white or wholemeal sliced bread

hundreds and thousands (multi-coloured)

METHOD

Butter the bread.

Sprinkle evenly with 1–2 teaspoons hundreds and thousands per slice.

Use a 4cm (1¾in) fluted cutter to cut out 3 circles and/or stars from each slice.

Arrange on paper-doily covered plates in pastel shades for maximum fairy appeal.

Peanut Butter and Jelly

When I first visited the USA in 1973 I was quite anxious about trying this all-time American favourite combination. I was expecting jelly, as in wobbly birthday party jelly, and the prospect was not appealing! When the day came, I was pleasantly surprised to be presented with a plateful of little crackers with a smear of peanut butter and a smear of mild-tasting and not oversweet smooth grape jam (jelly!) on top of each.

I have subsequently found peanut butter to be a delicious component in many unexpected but delicious sandwich pairings. Some of my favourites are: honey, banana, Vegemite, Marmite (quite a different thing), cucumber, sandwich spread, chicken (think satay) and Nutella.

MAKES 2 SANDWICHES

INGREDIENTS

4 slices wholemeal or white bread

1 tablespoon crunchy peanut butter

1 tablespoon strawberry or grape jam/jelly, (ideally this needs to be lump free and not too sweet)

METHOD

Generously spread 2 slices of fresh bread with peanut butter,

Spread the other two slices with a thin layer of the chosen jam/jelly.

Place the two halves together, cut into four triangles and serve.

Tiger Toast (left)
Jam and Banana Sandwich (above)

Tiger Toast

The Vegemite (or Marmite) and cheese combination is another unexpected treat. Everyone has their own preference for thickness of the Vegemite spread, but it's also important for this sandwich that the cheese has sufficient flavour to balance the salty strength of the Vegemite.

MAKES 4 SLICES OF TOAST

INGREDIENTS

4 slices sliced wholemeal bread
butter
Vegemite (or Marmite)
2 square cheese slices (25g, ¾oz each)

METHOD

Toast the fresh bread lightly. It is important not to overbrown as it will be going back under the grill later.

Spread with butter and then Vegemite in an even layer.

Cut the cheese slices horizontally into five strips and arrange into stripes on top of the vegemite toast.

Put under the grill and cook until cheese has melted.

Jam and Banana Sandwich

This sandwich is a picnic favourite from my childhood.

MAKES 2 SANDWICHES

INGREDIENTS

4 slices wholemeal bread
butter
1 tablespoon raspberry jam
1 banana
lemon juice

METHOD

Butter each slice of fresh bread.

Spread two slices with jam.

Slice the banana quite thickly and cover the jam using lines of three slices per row. Squeeze over a little lemon juice, this prevents the banana from excessive browning but also adds a lovely zingy flavour.

Lay the top slice of fresh bread on top of the banana and press down firmly.

Cut the sandwich in two horizontally, trying to preserve whole banana slices if possible as these are more likely to stay inside the bread.

Picnic Sandwich

This snack became a firm favourite in my circle of friends as the 'points' value of the corn cakes made them a dieter's dream. I'm sure the peanut butter and chocolate spread are not. However, this really does taste like a chocolate bar, has much fewer calories and provides welcome relief from any diet when served with a nice cup of tea. Children love them too!

MAKES 2

INGREDIENTS

4 corn cakes/thins
1 teaspoon crunchy peanut butter
1 teaspoon chocolate/hazelnut spread (Nutella)

METHOD

Spread two corn cakes with peanut butter and two with chocolate spread.

Press together.

Enjoy!

Ham and Cheese Fingers

A slightly upmarket toasted cheese sandwich. Children love the oozy cheese and the flattened bread makes it compact, easy to eat and deliciously warming. These are also very quick and easy to make, which makes them perfect for parties and spontaneous snacks.

MAKES 20 FINGERS

INGREDIENTS

1 whole Turkish flat bread
butter
10 slices (25g, ¾oz each) tasty cheese
10 slices of ham (approx 200g/6½oz)

METHOD

Split the Turkish fresh bread horizontally and butter each side.

Cover the whole of one side with cheese slices and then with ham slices.

Place the top layer back on the cheese and ham and cut in half or thirds.

Place the large sandwich(es) onto a heated sandwich press for approx 4 minutes or until cheese is melted.

Allow to cool slightly, then cut each half into 5 fingers and down the middle to make 10. Repeat with each section.

Serve with tomato wedges or tomato sauce for dipping.

Mini Burgers

Everyone is serving mini burgers at parties as they provide a meal in the hand. The mini 'bake at home' rolls from the supermarket provide the perfect size and torpedo shape to hold the ingredients.

MAKES 8

INGREDIENTS

1 small onion, very finely chopped

250g (8oz) beef mince

2 beef stock cubes

salt and pepper

8 mini baguettes/rolls

1 tablespoon tomato sauce

8 small lettuce leaves (baby cos or salanova lettuces have bite-sized leaves which are perfect), plus extra for garnish

4 cherry tomatoes, sliced into 4

8 baby beetroot slices (optional)

1 tablespoon mayonnaise (see Condiments)

5–6 cornichons, sliced thinly (optional)

METHOD

Gently cook the onions until soft, then allow to cool.

Combine mince, cooled onions and crumbled (dry) stock cubes and mix together well. Season with salt and pepper.

Divide the mixture into 8 and roll each portion into a ball. Squash slightly to flatten into a burger or sausage shape (depending on the shape of the bread roll you are using).

Shallow fry (or grill) the burgers for approximately 4 minutes on each side, ensuring that they are browned on the outside and cooked through.

If using cook-at-home rolls, bake them in the oven according to the packet instructions.

Split the rolls in half, keeping the halves attached, and spread the tomato sauce on one side.

Put the cooked burgers inside the rolls.

Layer the lettuce, tomato, beetroot and top with a blob of mayonnaise and a few slices of cornichon.

Serve on a large platter garnished with mini lettuce leaves.

Ice Cream Sandwich

These are a quick and easy dessert treat that adults and children enjoy equally. Up the ante by using sophisticated flavours of ice cream and making the biscuits and/or the ice cream from scratch.

MAKES 9

INGREDIENTS

1 packet chocolate-coated wheatmeal biscuits
9 scoops vanilla or chocolate ice cream

METHOD

Prepare the ice cream by scooping into a large tray and working it so that it is approximately 2cm (1in) thick and slightly softened.

Lay a biscuit, chocolate side down, onto the ice cream and cut around it neatly, making a vertical edge. Lift the biscuit and ice cream together out of the tray and sandwich together with the second biscuit. Press slightly to stick the biscuits together.

Neaten the edges using a knife or your (clean) fingers, if easier.

These can be served as is, or you can roll the finished sandwich ice cream edge through some chopped nuts or chocolate vermicelli, or place smarties or other chocolate-y sweets around the circumference for a more decorative effect. Work quickly though as the ice cream will be melting.

On a hot day, place in the freezer for 10 minutes to firm up. Otherwise serve immediately with plenty of serviettes.

Serve Yourself Wraps

Children really enjoy the independence of selecting their own ingredients in these wraps. And end up eating vegetables they would not normally eat!

Start with a variety of wraps: burritos/sorj/spinach/wholemeal/circular/square/mountain bread etc. Add a range of bowls with prepared vegetables and other fillings, for example: grated cheese, grated carrot, sultanas, shredded iceberg lettuce, chopped tomatoes, cucumber cubes, shredded ham, tuna, pineapple pieces, shredded cabbage.

Let them select condiments: mayonnaise, tomato sauce, sweet chilli sauce, or Kecap manis (sweet soy sauce).

These filled wraps can be served whole or sliced into two, four or six depending on the size of sandwich you want or number of mouths to be fed. They are also great for parties!

Cheese and Salad Wrap

INGREDIENTS

100g (3½oz) tasty cheese, grated

2 carrots, grated

shredded iceberg lettuce

1 tomato, finely diced

1 cucumber, finely diced

1 tablespoon (20ml) mayonnaise (see Condiments)

a packet of wraps

salt and pepper

METHOD

Finely slice and dice all salad ingredients.

Spread mayonnaise onto wrap.

Carefully arrange all ingredients in a line on the bottom third of the wrap and season.

Wrap tightly and place edge down.

Slice diagonally into quarters and arrange on tray.

Tuna, Sweet Corn, Lettuce and Mayonnaise Wrap

INGREDIENTS

350g (11½oz) tin of sweet corn (or frozen corn)

large (425g, 14oz) tin of tuna

2 tablespoons (30ml) good quality egg mayonnaise (see Condiments)

2 teaspoons (10ml) soy sauce

salt and black pepper

½ shredded iceberg lettuce

a packet of wraps

METHOD

Combine corn, tuna and mayonnaise.

Add soy sauce and seasoning to taste.

Place a line of filling and shredded lettuce along the bottom third of the wrap.

Wrap tightly and place edge down.

Slice diagonally into thirds and arrange on tray.

Chinese Chicken Wrap

INGREDIENTS

2 teaspoons (10ml) hoisin sauce

2 teaspoons (10ml) soy sauce

a packet of wraps

½ Chinese cabbage, finely shredded

3 shallots, julienned

1 long cucumber, julienned

a handful of beansprouts

4 chicken thigh fillets (prepared as in recipe page 165), shredded

METHOD

Mix together the hoisin and soy sauces.

Spread each wrap thinly with the sauce.

Slice and shred all salad ingredients and combine.

Mix shredded chicken thigh meat through salad ingredients.

Carefully arrange mixed ingredients in a line on the bottom third of the wrap.

Wrap tightly and place edge down.

Slice diagonally into quarters and arrange on tray.

Ham, Cheese and Pineapple Wrap

INGREDIENTS

4 thick slices (approx 100g, 3½oz) leg ham, chopped into chunks

½ small tin (125g/4oz) pineapple chunks, drained and finely chopped

1 tablespoon mayonnaise (see Condiments)

1 tablespoon milk

¼ iceberg lettuce

100g (3½oz) tasty cheese, grated

salt and black pepper

a packet of wraps

METHOD

Mix the chopped leg ham and crushed pineapple together.

Thin the mayonnaise with a small quantity of milk.

Shred the iceberg lettuce finely and combine with the ham and pineapple. Add the cheese.

Coat all ingredients gently with the mayonnaise. Season with salt and pepper.

Carefully arrange ingredients in a line on the bottom third of the wrap.

Wrap tightly and place edge down.

Slice diagonally into quarters and arrange on tray.

Something for a Picnic

In our house, we are usually in a rush to leave for a day out and trying to remember all the last-minute things we always forget: napkins, wine glasses, something to sit on. A picnic sandwich can be prepared well in advance and easily adapted to suit all tastes. The picnic loaf is incredibly easy and also very impressive. It actually tastes and presents better if made the day before, leaving the day of the picnic free for other preparations. Wraps are also excellent, as they can be laid side by side in a large plastic container that holds them in shape, and layered between sheets of baking paper. Beware of making wraps too far in advance as they can become soggy if they contain salad ingredients.

For a satisfying and delicious picnic, I would suggest choosing just two of the recipes (or your other favourite sandwiches) and making plenty of them. Supplement these with a delicious pre-made green salad (take the dressing in a sealed jar or container to pour over at the last minute) or coleslaw, some tomatoes that can be sliced and drizzled with olive oil and balsamic vinegar before leaving home, and a large wedge of your favourite cheese to serve with crackers and fruit. You can also add some pre-made nibbles—chips, nuts, fresh breadsticks—for grazing. Perfect!

Don't forget the knife! And something to sit on!

Layered Picnic Loaf

SERVES 6–8

INGREDIENTS

1 round loaf, white or wholemeal but must have a thick and sturdy crust

100g (3½oz) cream cheese, softened

2 tablespoons (30ml) mayonnaise (see Condiments)

100g (3½oz) feta cheese

1/2 bunch flat-leaf parsley or basil or coriander leaves or a combination of these

a selection of chargrilled/roasted vegetables (e.g. capsicum, pumpkin, carrot, eggplant, sweet potato zucchini, tomatoes, onion, garlic)

1/2 packet baby spinach or rocket leaves-2 handfuls

salt and black pepper

smoked/cured meat: choose one from prosciutto, Parma ham, braesola etc (optional) (approx 12 slices.)

METHOD

Slice a 3–4cm (1–2in) lid off the top of the loaf and scoop out the fresh bread to approximately 2cm (¾in) thickness all around.

Combine the cream cheese with the mayonnaise and spread a thick layer of the mixture onto the bottom of the loaf. Sprinkle with half the crumbled feta cheese.

Place a layer of basil leaves, followed by a layer of the vegetables. Repeat. Make sure that you cover each layer with a full layer of the vegetables to ensure that each bit of the loaf has the same combination of ingredients.

Finish the vegetable layer with spinach or rocket leaves and press down slightly to compact.

Season well with salt and pepper.

Add a layer of cold meat—approx 4 slices per layer.

The loaf needs to be filled to the brim so continue to layer ingredients until you reach the top of the fresh bread crust case.

Spread the remaining cream cheese/mayonnaise on top of the last vegetable layer.

Sprinkle on the remaining feta cheese and flat-leaf parsley or basil leaves.

Lay down a final layer of spinach or rocket leaves to seal all the ingredients below.

Replace the lid and wrap the loaf tightly in aluminium foil. Refrigerate for at least 1 hour to allow the ingredients to set and flavour each other.

Serve by cutting into wedges.

Nicoise Baguette

The nicoise salad is a beautiful combination of strong flavours that just work together so well. This sandwich combines the main elements of a Nicoise into a filling for a whole baguette, which can then be wrapped, refrigerated or immediately transported on a picnic for cutting up on location.

SERVES 6–10

INGREDIENTS

30 green beans, chopped into 3cm (1in) lengths

2 hard-boiled eggs

½ teaspoon balsamic vinegar

2 tablespoons (30ml) mayonnaise (see Condiments)

1 large tin (425g, 14oz) of good tuna chunks, drained

1 tablespoon capers, finely chopped

8 cherry tomatoes, quartered

10-15 black olives (pitted)

salt and pepper

1 long baguette (French or sourdough is best)

butter

mixed leaves

METHOD

Cook the beans by boiling in water for approximately 4 minutes. As soon as they are cooked (still bright green and crisp but softened), refresh in cold water. This retains the vibrant green colour and keeps them crisp.

Chop each egg into 8 pieces.

Mix the balsamic vinegar into the mayonnaise.

Combine the cooled beans with the tuna, egg, capers, olives, tomatoes and mayonnaise. stirring carefully to avoid breaking it into a sloppy paste. Season to taste.

Split the baguette in half lengthways and spread each side lightly with butter.

Spread the mixture along the whole length of the baguette.

Top with mixed leaves and the other half of the baguette.

Wrap tightly in plastic wrap or foil until required.

Chop into sections as needed; will serve 6 people generously or 10 as part of a meal.

Chicken and Coriander Wrap

MAKES 6

INGREDIENTS

6 wraps (burrito style)

4 tablespoons (60ml) mayonnaise (see Condiments)

1 bunch coriander leaves and stalks, chopped (reserve some unchopped for garnish)

2 teaspoons ground coriander

1 lime

salt and pepper

2 chicken breasts, poached or pan-fried

1 shredded iceberg lettuce

METHOD

Combine the mayonnaise with both the fresh and ground coriander.

Add the grated zest and juice of half the lime. Season to taste.

Add the cooked shredded chicken to the mayonnaise and turn gently to coat.

Place a line of shredded lettuce along the bottom third of the wrap and top with a line of half of the chicken and mayonnaise.

Roll tightly and wrap in plastic wrap/foil.

Serve with large sprigs of fresh coriander and a lime wedge.

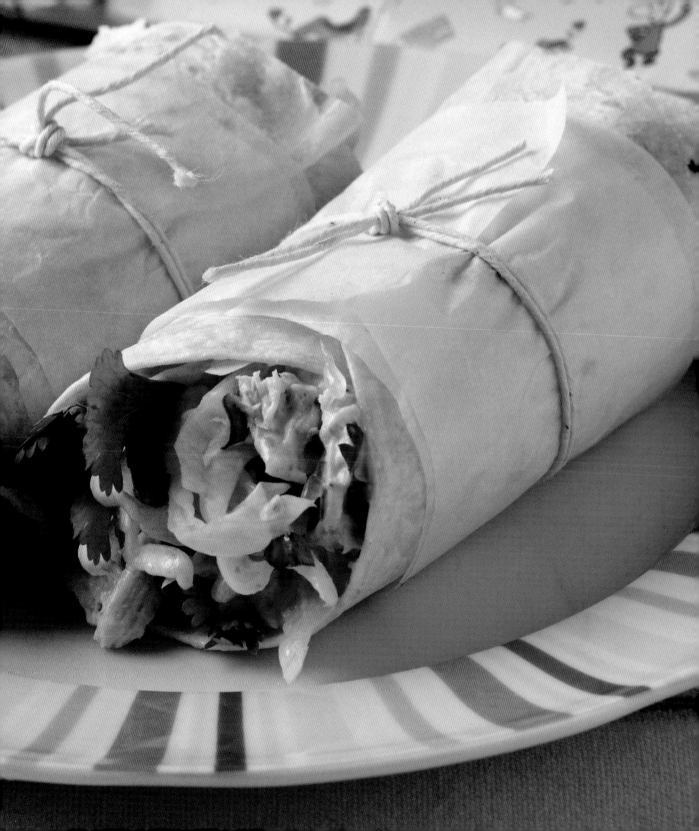

Five spice Honey Soy Chicken Wrap

MAKES 6

INGREDIENTS

500g (1lb) chicken thigh fillets (or substitute ½ Chinese duck)

2 tablespoons honey

4 tablespoons soy sauce

2 tablespoons kecap manis

2 teaspoons five-spice powder

1 tablespoon hoisin sauce

6 wraps (burrito style)

1 iceberg lettuce, shredded

1 cucumber, julienned

4 spring onions

METHOD

To cook the chicken thigh fillets, place them in a large roasting tin and flatten them out.

Mix together honey, soy sauce, kecap manis and five-spice powder. Pour over the chicken and coat well. Leave to marinate for half an hour if you have time.

Cover with foil and cook in a high oven for about 40 minutes, removing the foil and cooking uncovered for an extra 10 minutes at the end. This allows the chicken to develop some crispy edges.

When cooked and slightly cooled, shred into chunks.

Combine an extra tablespoon of kecap manis and hoisin sauce.

Put a generous smear of sauce in a line on each wrap.

Add the shredded chicken in a line and top with the lettuce, cucumber and spring onion.

Wrap tightly and cut into two on the diagonal.

Wrap in foil and transport tightly packed so that the wraps don't unroll.

Middle Eastern Sandwich

SERVES 2

INGREDIENTS

4 slices of wholemeal fresh bread

1 tablespoon hoummous (see Condiments)

4 x jarlsberg cheese slices (25g/1oz each)

approximately 8 slices salami

1 tomato, sliced

salt and black pepper=

METHOD

Spread two slices of fresh bread generously with hoummous.

Place 2 cheese slices on the hoummous and top with salami slices.

Add tomato slices and season well with salt and pepper.

Wrap well in plastic wrap or foil to transport.

Prosciutto, Gorgonzola and Fig Roll

INGREDIENTS

2 rosetta rolls or similar crusty bread roll

8 slices of prosciutto

4 slices (100g/3½oz) of gorgonzola cheese

2 fresh figs, sliced

salt and black pepper

balsamic vinegar (aged) and olive oil to drizzle

METHOD

Split the rolls in half horizontally and layer the prosciutto and cheese abundantly.

Add 1 whole fig, in slices, to each roll.

Season with salt and pepper, drizzle with sweet balsamic vinegar and olive oil.

Wrap in foil.

Chicken, Avocado and Artichoke Rolls

SERVES 2

INGREDIENTS

½ avocado, mashed with a dash of lemon juice

1 cooked chicken breast

1 tablespoon mayonnaise (see Condiments)

salt and black pepper

4 artichoke hearts, chopped

2 wholemeal soft rolls

¼ iceberg lettuce

METHOD

Spilt the roll in half horizontally and spread with mashed avocado.

Shred the cooked chicken finely and mix it gently (to avoid making a paste) with the mayonnaise, salt and pepper.

Chop the artichoke hearts into small pieces.

Divide the chicken between the two rolls. Top with finely shredded lettuce and artichoke pieces.

Top with the other half of the roll.

Hearty
and
Healthy

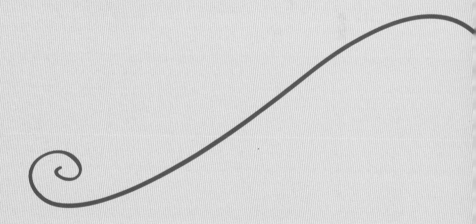

Some sandwiches should be all about the contents, while others rely on an artful combination of the flavours within and the bread used to encase them. The sandwiches that follow are my personal favourites and are specifically about the bread.

It's All About the Bread

BEM

BEM stands for bacon, egg and mayonnaise, a creamier take on bacon, lettuce and tomato.

MAKES 2 ROLLS

INGREDIENTS

2 wholemeal soft round rolls

2 eggs, hard-boiled

I tablespoon (20ml) mayonnaise (see Condiments)

salt and black pepper

6 rashers of short/middle bacon or 2 slices leg ham off the bone

baby rocket leaves or lettuce leaves, to garnish

METHOD

Halve the rolls horizontally.

Slice the hardboiled eggs and combine/mash with the mayonnaise using a fork.

Season well with salt and pepper.

Cook the bacon until turning crisp. Blot with kitchen paper to remove excess fat.

Divide the egg mixture between the rolls. Top with bacon.

Assemble with second half of roll.

Serve with some baby rocket or lettuce leaves on the side.

New Yorker on Rye

SERVES 2

INGREDIENTS

butter

4 slices dark rye bread

2 tablespoons Thousand Island dressing (see Condiments)

4 slices corned beef

1½ cups coleslaw, (see Condiments) plus extra for garnish

2 slices (50g, 1½oz) Swiss cheese (jarlsberg, gouda, edam)

METHOD

Lightly butter each slice of bread and work with the buttered sides outwards.

Spread the Thousand Island dressing on the unbuttered side of each slice of bread.

Place the corned beef, then the coleslaw, and then the cheese on top of the dressing on two slices.

Place the other slices on top with the dressing side down, buttered side out.

Place buttered side down on a preheated griddle or use a sandwich press.

Heat the sandwich until fresh bread is golden brown.

Cut the sandwich in half and serve with extra coleslaw (and fries!).

Avocado, Pesto and Tomato on Sourdough

Avocados and tomatoes offer a great combination of vitamins, good oils and plenty of flavour. You can use the bread as is and assemble as a sandwich, but I prefer the extra crunch and flavour offered by toasting the bread and rubbing a cut garlic clove over it.

SERVES 2

INGREDIENTS

4 slices multigrain (or white) sourdough bread

1 garlic clove, cut in half

2 tablespoons pesto (see Condiments)

1 avocado, thickly sliced

2 tomatoes, finely sliced

chicken salt or salt and pepper

olive oil

basil leaves (optional)

METHOD

Toast all the bread. Rub a cut garlic clove over one side of each slice.

Spread each slice of toast with pesto. Slice or roughly mash the avocado (half for each person) on each slice of fresh bread. Top with the sliced tomato and season well.

Drizzle with olive oil.

Add torn basil leaves if desired.

Slice in half and serve immediately.

Really Healthy Salad Roll

It is the combination of sweet, leafy, earthy and very savoury flavours that distinguish a good salad sandwich from a very ordinary one.

INGREDIENTS

2 wholemeal bread rolls (sesame-seed topped rolls are good for extra texture and flavour)

butter

1 tablespoon (20ml) mayonnaise (see Condiments)

50g (1½oz) grated tasty or cream cheese (optional)

Mixed leaves (it is good to include rocket as this adds a lovely pepperiness)

2 tomatoes, sliced

½ Lebanese cucumber, sliced

4 slices beetroot (can use fresh or tinned)

alfalfa/snow pea sprouts/cress/watercress

1 carrot, grated

salt and black pepper

METHOD

Spread both halves of the roll with butter and only one with mayonnaise. Spread the other half with cream cheese if using.

Begin with the leaves, top with tomato, cucumber slices, beetroot, sprouts or cress then grated carrot.

Add tasty cheese, if using.

Season well with lots of salt and ground black pepper.

Turkey, Brie and Cranberry on Sourdough

MAKES 2

INGREDIENTS

butter

4 slices of white sourdough bread

2 teaspoons (10ml) mayonnaise

4 slices (approx 100g, 3½oz) cooked turkey breast

2 teaspoons cranberry jelly/sauce

50g (1½oz) brie or similar soft cheese (white castella, camembert etc.), thinly sliced

12 baby spinach leaves

salt and black pepper

METHOD

Butter two slices of fresh bread and spread the mayonnaise on the other slices.

Place the turkey on the mayonnaise side and then spread cranberry jelly on top.

Top with cheese slices.

Add spinach leaves and season well.

Top with second slice of fresh bread and cut in half to serve.

Smoked Ham, Jarlsberg and Tomato Chutney on Rye

Rye bread can be quite strongly flavoured and needs the fillings to match. The smoked ham and nutty cheese can take the robust tomato chutney without being overpowered.

SERVES 2

INGREDIENTS

butter

4 slices thickly cut rye bread

2 slices (approx 50g, 1½oz) smoked ham

2 slices (approx 50g, 1½oz) jarlsberg cheese

2 tablespoons tomato chutney (see Condiments)

salt and black pepper

tomato slices, to garnish

METHOD

Butter each slice of bread.

Layer the ham and cheese on two slices of the fresh bread and spread tomato chutney generously on the other two slices.

Season with salt and freshly ground black pepper.

Put the two slices together. Cut in half to serve, garnished with a couple of tomato slices.

Ploughmans on Crusty

A Ploughman's Lunch is served in almost every English pub using regional cheese, beer and/or cider. This version simplifies the essential ingredients into a tasty sandwich. Vitally important is a napkin and a knife.

SERVES 2

INGREDIENTS

½ baguette, cut into 2 pieces and split in half lengthways, still attached

butter

3–4 lettuce leaves

6 slices cucumber

1 tomato, sliced

50g (1½oz) strongly flavoured cheddar or tasty cheese

¼ red onion, finely sliced

Watercress or mustard cress 6 pickled onions

1 apple

1 tablespoon brown (Branston) pickle

METHOD

Spread the baguette with butter on each side.

Place lettuce leaves on bottom piece.

Put slices of cucumber and tomato on top.

Slice or crumble in half the cheese to each baguette.

Sprinkle with chopped red onion and cress.

Serve with 2 or 3 pickled onions, half of a sliced apple and a dish of brown/Branston pickle.

Ham, Pickles and Cheddar on Grain

Choose the seed/grain bread you like best. Go for a variety of seeds and try lots of different combinations of pickles to see which complement the breads best. Sesame, poppy, sunflower and pumpkin seeds are all good options. I like the maltiness of granary bread with the cheese and ham combination.

TO MAKE 2 SANDWICHES

INGREDIENTS

4 slices of richly textured seed bread

butter

2 generous slices (approx 50g, 1½oz) mature cheddar cheese

2 thick slices (approx 50g, 1½oz) of leg ham (off the bone)

1–2 teaspoons Branston pickle/piccalilli/cornichons/mustard pickles per sandwich, plus extra for garnish

mixed leaves, for garnish

METHOD

Spread each slice of fresh bread lightly with butter.

Top two slices with cheese and ham.

Spread the pickles onto the other slice and press the two slices together.

Serve with mixed leaves and extra pickles on the side.

Hot Sandwiches

BLT and Aioli

Bacon, lettuce and tomato sandwiches are filling and healthy. Add the aioli for extra taste.

MAKES 2 SANDWICHES

INGREDIENTS

4 rashers short (middle) bacon

4 slices wholemeal or white bread, from a square loaf

1 tablespoon aioli (see Condiments)

2 tomatoes, sliced

¼ iceberg lettuce, shredded

salt and black pepper

mixed leaves, to garnish

tomato wedges, to garnish

METHOD

Cook the bacon in a frying pan or grill, blot with kitchen paper to remove excess fat.

Toast the fresh bread lightly and spread each slice with the aioli (for extra punch, rub a cut, raw garlic clove over the toast).

Place bacon, tomato slices and shredded lettuce, in that order, on the aioli.

Season with salt and pepper.

Top with second slice of toast.

Cut in half on the diagonal and serve with a side of dressed mixed leaves and tomato wedges

Cheese Dreams

MAKES 2 SANDWICHES

INGREDIENTS

2 eggs

salt and pepper

4 slices white or wholemeal bread, buttered

4 slices (100g, 3½oz) tasty or Cheddar cheese

olive oil

mixed leaves, to garnish

cucumber or carrot sticks, to garnish

METHOD

Beat the eggs and season with salt and pepper.

Assemble the sandwich by putting together two slices of buttered fresh bread with two slices of cheese per sandwich.

Dip each sandwich into the egg mixture and turn over so both sides are well coated with egg.

Gently place eggy sandwich into a pre-heated frying pan with a little coating of olive oil. Fry gently until golden brown and then turn and cook the other side.

Cut the cooked sandwich in half (the cheese should be oozy and warm) and serve with some mixed leaves or cucumber/carrot sticks.

Ham, Cheese and Tomato Toastie on Turkish

INGREDIENTS

½ loaf Turkish bread

4 slices (approx 100g, 3½oz) Fontina/taleggio cheese

4 slices (approx 100g, 3½oz) good quality leg ham (off the bone)

2 tomatoes, sliced

olive oil, to drizzle

salt and pepper

a handful of rocket to garnish

balsamic vinegar, to drizzle

METHOD

Split the bread horizontally.

Lay cheese slices and ham along the length of the bottom of the bread.

Lay tomato slices on top, drizzle with olive oil and season well with salt and pepper.

Press in a sandwich press in one or two pieces. Cook for approximately 4 minutes, or until cheese is melting.

Serve with rocket drizzled with balsamic vinegar and olive oil.

Pressed Pizza

These pizzas are quick and easy. Because they are cooked in a sandwich press, they are a convenient snack for children to make independently. Just be aware that the thinner breads are quite fragile when loaded with hot cheese and tomato sauce and need to be handled with care.

MAKES 2 PIZZAS

INGREDIENTS

2 Lebanese bread/flat breads

1 tablespoon sugo (tomato sauce/paste) (see Condiments)

mushrooms, red capsicum, ham, black olives, basil leaves, very finely sliced (all optional)

2 handfuls (approximately 50g, 1½oz) grated mozzarella cheese

olive oil

salt and black pepper

METHOD

Lightly spread each piece of bread with sugo.

Add any of the listed ingredients on one half of the fresh bread and top liberally with grated mozzarella cheese.

Drizzle lightly with olive oil and season with salt and pepper.

Fold the bare half over the fillings and place on a heated sandwich press.

Cook for 3–4 minutes until tomato paste and cheese is melting out of the pizza.

Remove from the grill, cut into pieces and serve immediately.

Egg, Bacon and Cheese Muffin

This makes for a great hangover cure!

SERVES 2

INGREDIENTS

2 English muffins

4 slices short bacon

2 eggs

2 slices (50g, 1½oz) tasty cheese

salt and pepper

METHOD

Split the muffins in half and toast on the open side. Keep warm.

Cook the bacon in a frying pan or grill. Blot excess fat on kitchen towel.

Fry two eggs, ensuring that the top of the yolk is cooked but not hard.

Assemble cheese slice, bacon and egg on one side of each of the muffins. Season, top with the other half of the muffin and put in a heated sandwich press for two minutes.

Serve with tomato juice or a Bloody Mary.

Tuna Melt

INGREDIENTS

small tin (250g, 8oz) of tuna, drained

½ red onion, finely chopped

1 tablespoon (20ml) mayonnaise (see Condiments)

salt and black pepper

4 slices of wholemeal bread

25g (¾oz) cheese, grated

mixed leaves, for garnish

METHOD

Break up the tuna chunks and mix with the chopped onion and mayonnaise.

Season with salt and pepper.

Toast all 4 slices of fresh bread.

Share the tuna mixture evenly over each slice and top with grated cheese.

Grill for a couple of minutes until the cheese is golden and bubbling.

Garnish with mixed leaves.

Chip Butty

The best chip butties are made with chips from a fish and chip shop! The unique flavour of a traditional chip butty is no accident: proper chips are cooked in beef fat (dripping) and it is this flavour imparted to the butty that makes it so successful. However, good chips can be made at home by following the recipe below.

MAKES 2 BUTTIES

INGREDIENTS

2 large potatoes

vegetable oil, for frying

soft white bread roll (not crusty)

butter

salt

malt vinegar

tomato sauce (optional)

METHOD

Make the chips: peel the potatoes and cut into evenly shaped 1cm (1/3in) slices. Chop each slice into 4 sticks.

Rinse the chips in cold running water and dry thoroughly.

Heat the vegetable oil in a small pan. Test the temperature by dropping 1 chip into the oil. If it rises immediately to the surface with a coating of bubbles, the oil is ready. Cook the chips briefly (approx 3–4 minutes) until they begin to turn golden brown.

Drain the chips (keeping the oil) and set aside. Keep the oil on a very low heat.

Split the roll into two horizontally and butter each side.

Recook the chips in hot oil for 2–3 minutes. This will ensure their crispness and lightness inside.

Drain the chips on absorbent paper and salt well.

Pile them into the roll and sprinkle with malt vinegar.

Add tomato sauce if required.

Serve with surplus chips on the side.

Chip Butty

Breakfast Wrap

Breakfast Wrap

A transportable and convenient way of simulating the big breakfast, which also reduces the calorie count as the serving size is much smaller than a giant fry-up!

MAKES 2 SANDWICHES

INGREDIENTS

4 rashers middle bacon

2 large field mushrooms, thickly sliced

butter

1 large tomato, sliced

salt and pepper

2 eggs

olive oil

2 wraps (burrito style)

barbeque sauce

METHOD

Cook the bacon over a low heat in a frying pan or under a grill.

Drain on absorbent kitchen towel and keep warm in a low oven.

In the same pan, add a small knob of butter and the sliced mushrooms. Cook mushrooms for approximately 5 minutes until soft. Add to bacon.

Season the sliced tomato with salt and pepper and fry in the pan for approximately 2 minutes on each side. Keep warm with the bacon and mushrooms.

For the omelette, beat the eggs together and season with black pepper.

Heat a teaspoon of olive oil in the frying pan and pour in the beaten egg. Pull in the sides of the omelette with a spatula as the egg cooks and tip to fill the spaces until no egg runs loose.

Fold the omelette into thirds and cut lengthways in half.

Place egg onto the bottom part of the wrap. Drizzle sauce along the length of the egg.

Top with the still warm bacon, mushroom and tomato slices. Season well with salt and pepper.

Fold in the bottom end of the wrap to encase all the filling, then roll the wrap firmly. Secure with baking paper or a paper napkin.

Serve immediately.

Classic Steak Sandwich

INGREDIENTS

1 onion, sliced

olive oil

4 thick-cut slices crusty white bread

butter

2–3 iceberg lettuce leaves

1 tomato, sliced

2 teaspoons Dijon mustard

2 pieces (approximately 150g, 5oz each) New York cut/Porterhouse steak

lettuce, tomato and cucumber salad, to serve

fries, to serve on the side

METHOD

Cook the onion gently in olive oil to soften.

Prepare the bread by buttering one side of two slices and layering on the lettuce and tomato slices.

Spread the Dijon mustard on the other two slices.

Grill or pan-fry the steak to your liking, approximately 3 minutes on each side for medium rare. Leave to rest for at least 5 minutes.

Place rested steak on top of the salad ingredients. Top with cooked onion and the second slice of bread.

Serve with a small side salad of lettuce, tomato and cucumber and a side of fries.

American Club Sandwich

INGREDIENTS

I tablespoon (20ml) mayonnaise (see Condiments)

½ tablespoon Dijon mustard

6 slices wholemeal bread, toasted

4 iceberg lettuce leaves

4 slices (100g, 3½oz) tasty cheese

2 slices (25g, ¾oz) ham, thinly sliced

4 slices tomato

4 slices (25g, ¾oz) chicken or turkey breast, thinly sliced

4 slices cooked bacon (optional)

METHOD

Combine the mayonnaise and mustard and mix well.

Toast all 6 slices of fresh bread and spread each slice with a teaspoon of mayonnaise mixture.

On two pieces of toast, place a lettuce leaf, cheese slice, ham slice, 2 slices tomato and top with a second slice of toast, mayonnaise side down.

On top of the second slice of toast, place I slice of cheese, 2 slices of turkey, 2 slices of bacon and I lettuce leaf.

Finish each stack with the last slice of toast, mayonnaise side down.

Cut into triangles and secure with toothpicks.

Serve immediately with a large serviette.

Bacon Sandwich

Weekend breakfasts of my childhood were characterised by a bacon sandwich. The bacon needs to be generous in quantity and well-cooked, beginning to crisp with the fat rendering out and drained.

MAKES 2 SANDWICHES

INGREDIENTS

6 rashers middle bacon (rindless)
lard or dripping
4 slices thickly sliced soft white bread
tomato/barbecue/HP/Worcestershire sauce

METHOD

Fry the bacon in a shallow frying pan (no oil is needed) until beginning to crisp.

Remove the bacon from the pan, put on kitchen towel to absorb excess grease and keep warm.

Add a small knob of dripping or lard to the pan and dip the fresh bread, one side only, into the melted fat, ensuring that you pick up the burnt, salty flavours from the bacon cooking. (This replaces the butter and adds a truly rich and wonderful flavour.)

Assemble the sandwich, with 3 rashers per sandwich.

Serve with sauce of choice.

Croque Monsieur

A croque monsieur is a hot ham and cheese grilled sandwich. It originated in France as a fast food snack. More elaborate versions include the croque madame, the same recipe with a fried or poached egg on top, or with a mornay or béchamel sauce poured over.

SERVES 2

INGREDIENTS

2 croissants

2 slices (50g, 1¾oz) leg ham

2 slices emmental or gruyere cheese

METHOD

Split the croissant and layer in the ham and cheese slices.

Cook in a sandwich press for approximately 3 minutes or until the cheese is melting. Be vigilant, as cooking time will vary depending on the butter content of the croissant.

Condiments and Accompaniments

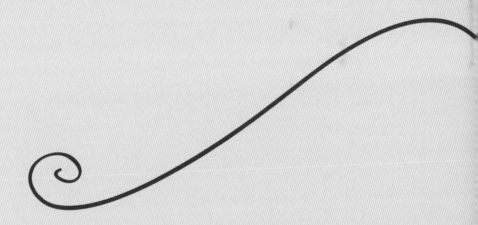

It is the small touches of additional flavour which elevate a simple sandwich from bread with filling to something really delicious. The following recipes provide those extra elements —sweet relishes, creamy dressings, spreads, crunchy vegetables and salads.

Mayonnaise

Making your own mayonnaise is extremely simple. Once made it stores well in the fridge for several days. The technique of blending is made much easier by mixing all the ingredients in a blender, as follows:

INGREDIENTS

1 whole egg

1 tablespoon Dijon or French mustard

1 tablespoon white balsamic, wine vinegar or lemon juice

salt to taste

300ml (10fl oz) vegetable or canola oil

METHOD

Combine the egg, mustard, vinegar/lemon juice and seasonings first and then add the oil. Whisk together until thick and creamy in colour and texture.

Alternatively, you can use a good store-bought whole egg mayonnaise, which is almost as good and has the added advantage of storing for much longer in the fridge once opened.

Flavoured Mayonnaise

Zest and juice of lemon and lime

Anchovies (2–4 anchovy fillets, finely chopped)

Chilli (flakes, powder or chopped fresh to your taste)

Mustards: whole grain, Dijon, Hot English

Herbs: coriander, mint, rosemary, thyme, dill, all work well

Ground spices: cumin, coriander, paprika, ginger, garam masala, curry powder

Vinegars: balsamic and other sweet vinegars are great

Grated (and squeezed) cucumber or other pureed vegetables

Or you can combine mayo with other pre-made sauces: tomato chutney, soy, sweet chilli, barbecue and good old tomato sauce

Aioli

To 2 tablespoons mayonnaise, add ½ clove of very finely crushed garlic, or roasted garlic, and mix together well.

Thousand Island Dressing

INGREDIENTS

1 cup (8oz) whole egg mayonnaise

1 cup (8oz) tomato sauce

¼ cup (2oz) sweet pickle relish

2 teaspoons Worcestershire sauce

1 tablespoon sugar

¼ cup (2fl oz) milk, (optional)

1 boiled egg, very finely chopped (optional)

METHOD

Combine all ingredients in a food processor/blender and mix until smooth.

Caramelised Onion Relish

INGREDIENTS

3 large brown onions

50g (1½ butter)

1 teaspoon oil

3 teaspoons balsamic vinegar

1½ tablespoons brown sugar

METHOD

Finely slice the onions.

Cook these in a mixture of butter and oil for at least 10 minutes until they are completely soft and beginning to go brown.

Add balsamic vinegar and brown sugar. Continue cooking for a further 10-20 minutes, adding a little water if needed.

Coleslaw

INGREDIENTS

¼ white cabbage

½ red onion

2 tablespoons mayonnaise

2 tablespoons milk

lemon juice (juice of ½ lemon)

1 apple, grated

1 carrot, grated

salt and black pepper

METHOD

Finely shred cabbage and onion.

Combine mayonnaise with milk and lemon juice—the mixture should be quite runny to coat the vegetables.

Combine all the ingredients, season with salt and pepper and mix well together.

Raspberry Jam

This is the easiest jam recipe ever! All you need is the same quantity of sugar to the amount of raspberries you are using. Because raspberry seeds contain natural pectin you do not need to use any artificial thickener.

MAKES 350G/11 OZ

INGREDIENTS

1 cup (8oz) raspberries (frozen are completely fine)

1 cup (8oz) sugar (I use caster sugar that has had a vanilla pod in it for a little extra specialness)

METHOD

Place the sugar in a shallow ovenproof bowl or tray and out into a warm oven (approx 180ffC, 350ffF) for 10 minutes.

Mash the raspberries in a large saucepan over a medium heat and bring to the boil.

Allow to boil rapidly for 1 minute, stirring continually.

Add the warmed sugar to the boiling raspberries, it should return very quickly to the boil. Be careful, everything is extremely hot!

Boil gently for at least 5 minutes until the jam is visibly thicker and begins to look like a gel.

Carefully pour into a sterilised jar and seal with a plastic cover while still hot to maximise freshness.

Tomato Chutney

MAKES 500ML/17 FL OZ

INGREDIENTS

1 kg (2lb) fresh tomatoes
1 clove of garlic, finely chopped
½ onion, finely chopped or sliced
2 teaspoons red wine vinegar
2 teaspoons brown sugar
½ teaspoon ground ginger
3 cloves
½ pear or apple, chopped
8 dried dates or 40g (1¼oz) other dried fruit
salt and pepper
½ teaspoon ground cinnamon
dash of Worcestershire sauce

METHOD

Peel the tomatoes by cutting a shallow cross into the skin at the bottom of each one and dropping into boiling water for approx 2 minutes. Remove from water when skin begins to peel. Leave to cool then remove skins and seeds. Chop fresh into small pieces.

Prepare all ingredients except for dried fruit and seasoning, and combine in a saucepan on the stove.

Cook gently for at least half an hour before adding dried fruit. Add a dash or 3 of Worcestershire sauce and ground cinnamon. Cook for a further 30 minutes until well combined and most of the liquid has evaporated.

Season to taste. You may need to add more sugar or vinegar to balance the flavours to taste.

Pesto

Pesto can be made with a variety of ingredients and is an extremely versatile ingredient. The herbs, nuts and cheese that form the critical basis of this delicious paste can be combined differently for diverse flavours.

The following quantities make a small batch of pesto that would serve 2–3 people mixed through hot pasta, or spread 8–10 slices of toast/rolls if making a sandwich. Fresh pesto does not keep very well so I prefer to make small batches when I need it. It takes no more than 5 minutes to make.

INGREDIENTS

½ bunch picked basil leaves (can also use coriander, mint, parsley)

2 tablespoons almonds (pine nuts are more traditional but I prefer the more subtle flavour of almonds, can also use brazil, hazelnuts, macadamias, pistachios)

25g (¾oz) Parmesan cheese, finely grated

½ cup (100ml, 3½fl oz) olive oil

salt

METHOD

Combine all dry ingredients in a mortar and pestle or food processor until well chopped. Add oil and mix well together. The consistency should be pasty and not too oily.

Season to taste.

Tomato Sauce

INGREDIENTS

1 brown onion, finely chopped

3 cloves of garlic, finely chopped

olive oil

2 tins chopped tomatoes (each 375g) (you can use fresh tomatoes if you prefer)

1 teaspoon sugar

a handful basil, oregano or flat-leaf parsley leaves, chopped (optional)

salt and black pepper

METHOD

Gently fry the onions and garlic in the olive oil over a low heat.

When softened and golden in colour, add the tomatoes and cook gently for at least 15 minutes until you have a thick, rich tomato sauce.

Add the fresh herbs and sugar at the end of cooking time. Season to taste.

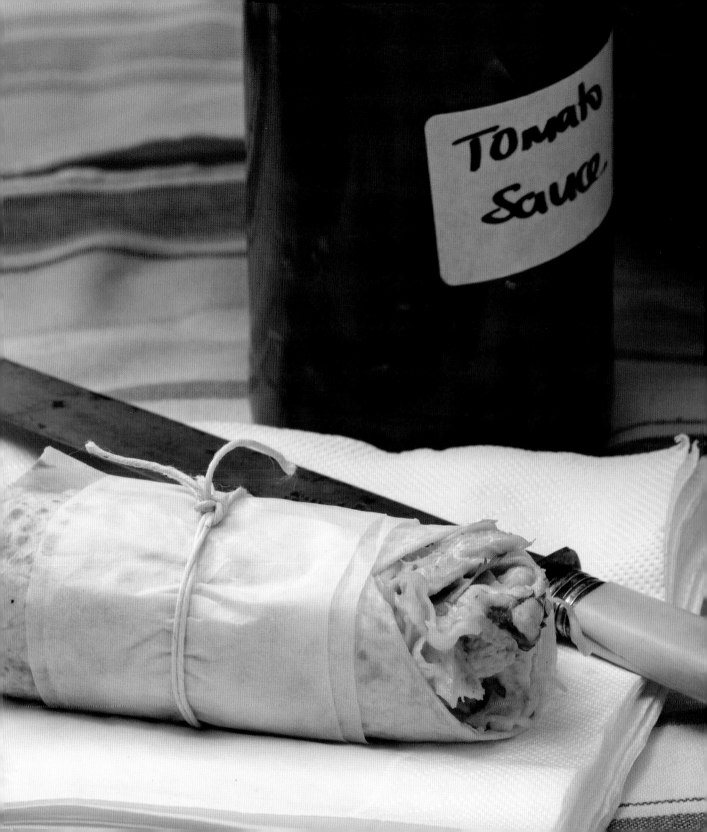

Hoummous

INGREDIENTS

400g (13oz) chickpeas
2 heaped teaspoons tahini
juice and zest of ½ a lemon
50ml (1¾fl oz) olive oil
½ teaspoon paprika
½ clove of garlic, crushed
½ teaspoon sea salt
1–2 tablespoons cold water (adjust according to the consistency you like)

METHOD

Blend all ingredients until they make a smooth paste. Add water as required.

Semi-dried Tomatoes

This is a great recipe to use up disappointing tomatoes that don't have as much flavour as you'd hoped, or those which are slightly past their best for presentation purposes.

INGREDIENTS

6-8 tomatoes

3 teaspoons oregano, leaves, dried

2 cloves garlic, finely chopped

salt and pepper

olive oil

METHOD

Quarter or eighth the tomatoes into wedges. Place them flesh side up on a baking sheet covered with baking/greaseproof paper. Sprinkle the tomatoes evenly with dried oregano leaves, finely chopped garlic, salt, pepper and a drizzle of olive oil.

Roast in a low oven for about 45 minutes.

Leave to cool, then store in a sealed container in the fridge, for up to a week.

Leaves and Garnishes

As with all ingredients, choose leaves that are fresh, in season and best complement the other flavours you are using. Lettuces and green leaves are not all the same.

Use iceberg lettuce when a crisp texture with a very subtle flavour is required. Cos lettuce is similarly crisp but has a slightly more bitter flavour, so offers a contrasting rather than a bland taste.

Use butter or salanova lettuces where a softer texture and less flavour are required. Salanova also have delightful miniature leaves, which look good for presenting food.

Spinach is great for colour and has a mild earthy flavour that particularly complements red meats and oily fish.

Rocket is a peppery leaf. Baby rocket is great for smaller sandwiches and the larger leaves can have a more intense flavour. Beware of the amount of leaves you use in any combination, as the flavour of rocket can be overpowering.

Chargrilled/Roasted Vegetables

Any vegetable can be reinvented by roasting it. They gain a sweetness, a nutty, caramelised quality which adds a delicious richness to their flavour.

Good vegetables to try are: cauliflower, broccoli, sliced zucchini, eggplant, sweet potato, onion wedges, celery and carrot sticks, pumpkin, beetroot, fennel, whole red and green capsicum.

Common pairings of vegetables with other ingredients include:

- Pumpkin and feta/goat's cheese
- Carrots and chicken
- Sweet potato and salmon or trout
- Broccoli and stilton (or any blue cheese)
- Cauliflower and cheddar-type cheeses
- Beetroot and goat's cheese/feta
- Fennel and meats, especially pork and lamb

Whole cloves of garlic (in their skins) also roast really well and can be used to flavour sauces and dressing as an ingredient in their own right.

METHOD

Preheat the oven to moderate heat. Prepare the vegetables you are using in a large roasting tin by cutting into similar sized chunks or slices to ensure even cooking. Smaller chunks generally would lead to a greater intensity of caramelisation since there is greater surface area, this may or may not be the flavour you are after!

Leave the skin on wherever possible as this improves the textural quality as well as adding flavour and nutrition.

Season well with salt and pepper.

Drizzle (or spray) with olive oil. If you like you can also add herbs: choose rosemary, thyme, oregano or marjoram for slightly stronger and robust flavours that can withstand the oven.

Cook for 40 minutes to 1 hour, depending on the size of pieces you have cut. Check regularly and turn once or twice to ensure even cooking and browning.

Roasted vegetables can be stored in an airtight container in the fridge for two or three days.

Potted Beef

This quantity of potted beef will make about 30 sandwiches, but you can also enjoy it as an excellent breakfast treat on toast or an accompaniment to a cheese board with some melba toast or baguette slices.

INGREDIENTS

400g (13oz) stewing or casserole beef

2 teaspoons anchovy essence, or 3 whole anchovy fillets

50g (1½oz) butter, cubed

salt and black pepper

METHOD

Cut the beef into small cubes and put into a large oven-proof saucepan or casserole dish with a lid.

Add three anchovy fillets and a little anchovy oil from the jar or tin.

Distribute cubed butter over the meat and cover with a tight-fitting lid.

Cook in a very low oven for at least 5 hours (or overnight) on a very low heat until all meat has broken down and can easily be separated.

Blend the cooled meat with a handheld blender or in a food processor until quite smooth.

Season with salt and black pepper. (Be careful when adding salt as the anchovies are salty.)

Put into a pot or jar with a lid and use as needed. Stores for up to a week in the fridge.

First published in Australia in 2010 by
New Holland Publishers (Australia) Pty Ltd
Sydney • Auckland • London • Cape Town

1/66 Gibbes Street Chatswood NSW 2067 Australia
218 Lake Road Northcote Auckland New Zealand
86 Edgware Road London W2 2EA United Kingdom
80 McKenzie Street Cape Town 8001 South Africa

A record of this book is held at the National Library of Australia

ISBN 9781742570785

Publisher: Lliane Clarke
Designer: Emma Gough
Illustrations: Lisa McKenzie
Photographs: Graeme Gillies
Food stylist: Kathy McKinnon
Kitchen assistant: Molly Blythin
Production Manager: Olga Dementiev
Printer: Toppan Leefung Printing (China) Ltd

10 9 8 7 6 5 4 3 2 1

Our thanks to Plenty Kitchen and Homewares, Victoire Bakery, Bakers Delight Rozelle